POEMS, SHORT STORIES, PICTURES, ALL IN AMBIT'S DOUBLE No. 200

AMBIT is edited by **Martin Bax** with **Mike Foreman** *(Art),* **Henry Graham** *(Poetry),* **Geoff Nicholson** *(USA Editor and Prose),* **Judy Bax** *(Financial Director),* **Tim Bax** *(Development),* **Travis Elborough** *(Marketing),* **Helen Gordon** *(Subscriptions),* **Emily Berry, Mike Smith** *(Editorial & Production),* **Helle Haakonsen, Guy Skelton** *(Editorial Assistants),* **John Morgan studio** *(Design)*

Corresponding Editors: **Carol Ann Duffy, Richard Dyer, Adam Ferner, Vanessa Jackson, Henry Lowther, Gwen MacKeith, Kate Pemberton, Ron Sandford, Satyendra Srivastava, Irving Wardle, Eugene Wolstenholme**

Ambit editorial address: 17 Priory Gardens, London N6 5QY, UK. Bookshop Distribution: Central Books / tel. 020 8986 4854. Printed by The Lavenham Press. See back flap for details of how to order a single copy or take out a subscription, or visit www.ambitmagazine.co.uk

AMBIT Issue 200, Spring 2010, ISSN 0002-6972. Selection © Ambit 2010. Copyright of individual pieces remains with contributors.

Illustration by Chris Pig

Peter Porter

A Toccatina of Galuppi's

O Galuppi, Baldassare, gone for good all Browning's praise,
Those commiserating sevenths, Music Theory's bad-hair days –
Lost are rhythm, assonances, apt conjunctions, gnomic phrase.

Hear the keyboard clatter coldly, cautious CDs sitting pretty –
Think the sunlight on Giudecca, haze above the golden city.
Wordless, Goethe, Corvo, Powell! Since the Futurists, who's witty?

Il Buranello yields to Nono, and the kissing's sternly stopped
The seven maids who for the Walrus and the carpenter once mopped
Have swept away by now the tearful sand on which the Frari's propped.

Bewildering your notes cascading through a handful of octaves.
The watertable at Marghera, falling, may expose the graves
And moonlight dousing the piazzas silver the advancing waves.

Past the Zattere, mud-churning, steepled Cruise Ships plumply dock.
The metronome, a silent convert, is attrition's ticking clock
And in San Bastian an expert marks down Veronese's stock.

San Zaccaria's great Bellini ponders Parsifal on tape
While Colleoni bumbles fiercely where Stravinsky lay in state.
Ateneo and Accademia authorise Europa's Rape.

What hangs in minor keys and major lingers in the mind like lead.
Those suspensions, those solutions – must we die? And then we're dead.
In the Ca' Rezzonica, one, Robert Browning, climbs to bed.

Poet in the sky with Diamonds

Magister to his Dog:
'What Do You Know About Kant?'

Here I hold the city plan of Königsberg
In my hand. This is one of those attempted
TV reconstructions using nothing
Not available in the heyday of the subject.
The clock was never late or ever previous;
Only the philosopher could be stranded
Out of time. Yet, was I? Perhaps
I was rehearsing the very moment
When my whole person would come to a stop.
Citizens, I seemed to say, if such
A mind as mine which I'm sure
You will hold more magnificently regular
Than yours, must collapse eventually
What can then be signified by The Laws
Of Creation, of which my appearance
On the stroke of a bell is only one
Calibration of everything being
Exactly and materialistically unchangeable,

There is no device, however Germanised,
Which can discountenance, for Philosophy's sake
Our being born later than Parmenides
And Plato: nor in the layers of future time
Will I have foreshortened any thought
Still to come, and this is why,
On breaking my morning steps, I dismayed
You all, having already disturbed my God.
But I cannot upset my dog who shares
This Universe with me – his 'walkies',
While unstructured beside mine, follow
A rustic metaphysics magical and natural,
So I demand of him, as his Master,
'What do you know about Kant?'
Which enfranchises the whole of Königsberg
To ask he same questions about their God.

The Long March of Cornelius Cardew

The hardest road, the hardiest foot on stone,
the unrolled bandage latticed with dried blood –
Great Truth alone can justify 4/4
We keep the palimpsestic scores in racks,
in hives of apian tyranny, the wax so soft
and yet so diligent, a thousand, more two thousand
years of pain notated by control,
the delta's varicose of a society
the which I said I loathed until
I heard Stockhausen damn it with
his apotheosis of Unhistory.
I knew at once his will was deathlier
than anything the Classics ever did,
the bead-games, tombs and truant nightingales.
If there were a Yangtse so immense
It dwarfed its river self, I know I'd hear
the left-right feet make music round
all temples, sepultures, stockyards, bus-stops,
a unison chromatically complete,
a march as fixed as hope, as long as sky.

I don't regret my absolutist scores,
at least they're beautiful to look at;
I am the son of a Ceramicist.
Someone saw Heaven once and it resembled
a circuit-board beyond Aldebaran,
panelled and personified, sure proof
that everything which is intelligent
waits its decay to only loveliness.
But still the march goes on. As always, the river
is beside us, its syncopated waves
a proper counterpoint to common time.
Already we have passed the brazen gate
Of Capitalism, obliging life to share
its dividends with us – if epic poetry
gives way to pleasant tunes, the reason is
it can't be sung downline; the city needs
to know the desert's proud intent,
that millions in their locust coats shall stand
beneath the walls of Old Metonymy,
and just one voice to magistrate the air.

Peter Porter is one of *Ambit*'s longest-standing contributors.
He has a new *Selected Poems* appearing in May from Picador.

The Generations

from the sketchbooks of Posy Simmonds

feel like a
procuress

Age of Innocence   Gentlemen
Ingenue   Gents

Dinner party: Frankie
♀ pregnant = all envaleur   Flora
♀ recently = covered up
delivered

vous savez que
en Angleterre on
s'appelle ça "The
pope's nose"
puisqu ce
qu'elle racont?

siff with laquer

false
eyelashes

backcombing
mouse's nest

1965?

gold
shoes
or satin
dyed to match?

central
zip?

blue eyeshade
scent Tiara?
Miss Dior

60s

cherry

1970's

flick-ups

patchwork

courtelle

duvet cover

cords

Russell &
Bromley
£28.99

£8.99
suede

70s

Tulip
chair

LoFt

Horrors of visiting
son + daughter in law.

Pop cube. side table

brickwork
painted white.

← bottom contoured

Hi Ply chains

spindly flimsy white

bare boards
everything on
the floor or low.

bed on the floor.

bloody furnitures
too low. you feel like
you're spatchcocked

80s

hair grip

enormous
bag

square-toed

round
roots

lace bolero

Smart car
full of balled-up
Kleenex

90s

Niqabs in Theobalds Rd

shiny cream

Busstop/King's X Rd

lipstick

pearl strings

fringed scarf

white

white stretchy

white sox

ballet shoes

white with frill

very glossy

rucksack

somali?
sudanese?
blue over
black, sometimes
sand/tan
over black

00s

Judy Gahagan

Moments in the Ark

With perhaps 100 months to go
I think of Noah's 40 days –
his three-floored Ark of gopher-wood
the two by two of living things
and humans plus their shadows
brought to float on a silent flood
shining and still as solid pewter –

and make of this moment now, my Ark,
my moment: shall not loveliness last forever?
For the chestnuts are lifting their tiers
into pink-white bridal May, over
the shining summer verges; the moment
held in that eighth day that lives
outside time, vast for the soul to rest in.

Noah, my ancient you lived 600 years
to reach that small room of great age and memory.
Did you have time to say goodbye
to the reeds and river pools, scarved girls standing
perennially like amphorae by the wells?

I too have had to say goodbye
to my beloved winter nights
the black-sheened bowls of them,
their heavens ful of chiselled stars
the ice-laced breath from the north,
from the Polar Zones of Inaccessibility.

In the moment of God's thunderbolt
you saw, we see, before the rains,
across the world colossal debris of high-rise
fossilised on martyred continents;
the refugees in stunted landscapes –
ruins, huts, shanties, filth, sores –
like hooded crows they'll caw ceaselessly
and above this world the fragment
of a reddish moon appears and
disappears among tumultuous clouds
like an anguished lantern.

Charles Shearer

But Noah, Jew, you'll have called your Ark
a teivah also meaning word
and in a word an image, time-stopped,
waterproofed against the dissolution
of all that ever held great beauty;
as soul stares out of the eyes of the starving
at an image of the loveliest ever dreamed.

At night, the Ark, a comfort zone
of eighth-day moments, floats
on a phantasmagoria of weird hopes;
comes to rest in yet another morning
light spilling from that mountain
across the water where Noah waited
and we float without progress
and wait like Noah
for the dove, for the sprig of green,
for the eternal Biblical rainbow.

Fog Stranger

Tonight the city has retreated into greys
faceless and nebulous as faith

the bridge beneath me metaphysical,
and a last cruiser casting silent

roils of thickly shining water
carries strangers who stare out at

nothing but the undertones
and the overtones of darkness visible.

The street lamps force down their light
I stare up till each light's a radiant web

filled in with fog; they are a line of patients
each eyeing the mystery of the other's sickness

that is aloneness. I remember the last
trains home crossing the bridges

the lights of strangers in their own homes
alone then as the city, now cut off

by fog, is alone, the buildings watchful.
They close in as if trying to hear

in the dense air, its silence, as under snow
it carries no sound so that the heart

protests at this being, not-being,
the terror of isolation, the terror of absorption,
each a kind of death, a disappearance
of self, not to dust but to this dark dew.

Judy Gahagan is a psychologist, translator,
poet, and prose writer. She's a tutor at the
Poetry School, London. Her verse biography
of Ludwig II of Bavaria, *Tours Around the Soul
of Ludwig*, was recently published in a bilingual
edition by Karl Stutz Verlag Passau.

Neighbours and Strangers

Carl Tighe

I had given up pretending to read and was snoozing in the late afternoon sunshine with my cat on my lap when the cat leapt away, over my shoulder, her claws digging into me for traction. In an instant she was wide-eyed, on a branch up a tree and there at the bottom was a black and white mongrel, snarling and snapping like some cartoon beast.

The dog's approach had been entirely silent. If the cat had not spotted it, she would almost certainly have been savaged where she slept, even while it slept on me. I wondered if it would be safe to get the hold of the dog's collar and lead it off, but while I was dithering, a boy aged about fourteen pushed through the hedge. He called the dog:
— Come on Robbie! It obeyed him instantly. A boy and his dog. Classic.
— Where do you live?
— Not from round here.
— I think your dog is a killer.
— He don't like cats.
— What's he doing in my garden anyway?
— Exploring.
— Why isn't he on a lead?
— He was only playing.
— My cat didn't think so.
— He didn't hurt it, just gave it a scare. The boy backed through the hedge, pulling the dog after him.
— Well, you keep him under better control in future, I called.
I spent the rest of the afternoon blocking the gap in the hedge and dabbing on ointment.

I had a surprise phone call from Orit. She was in Jerusalem. She said:
— I have finished with him. Boruch. A couple of months ago. So I was wondering if you would like to visit Israel for a few days. We could drive around a bit, see the country. I think you might like it…

She knew I would like it. She knew I liked her. She knew I would do nothing about it as long as she was with Boruch. I heard more than the promise of a drive in the country.

That summer I was teaching an English course for overseas students. I had an Israeli student called Ariel and a Palestinian student called Javid, both preparing to study at British universities. Ariel had come to Britain to study law — so at the first opportunity Javid asked me: why has he come here? There are dozens of law schools and universities offering law degrees in Israel. Javid, on the other hand, had come to Britain to study hydrology.

Why, Ariel asked me later the same day, is he here? Israel already makes the desert bloom, and besides there are good universities in Israel and in Palestine, so why should he travel all the way here to study?

Next morning Javid, the Palestinian student, insisted on telling me all about his family.

— My family name, Ja'far, it means priest, he began. Holy man. And when he had done telling me all about his beautiful sisters and their village he began to dish the dirt on the godless, land-jumping, pornography reading Israelis.

— You know they think only of making babies. They try to breed us out of our land now. And another thing — there is something wrong with that Israeli: he does not look like a Jew — blue eyes and blonde hair. So, I hear you are Irish. You know the Palestinians are the Irish of the Arab world. I want to invite you to come to my country. You will love it. You will see.

After we had checked into our hotel room Orit said:

— Let's go for a walk.

From her case she took a bullet proof vest and a pistol. She put on a denim jacket and buttoned it over the holster. She pulled her long blonde hair out from under the jacket so it flowed down her back. She looked very slim and golden in her jeans and jacket. The bulge of the gun hardly showed.

— Why do you look at me like that?

— I forgot you were once a soldier.

— I had no choice. Anyway, she said, patting the holster, it is not a bad thing to know how to use one of these things. Let's walk?

— Do you normally strap on a gun before you go for a walk.

— What is normal? Anyway, we are going through the old Arab market and there is some sort of strike action. You never know…

— What about me?

— What?

— Do I get a gun?

— You are not an Israeli. You are a tourist. And nominally at least, you are a Christian. So you are not in this war. You don't need one.

— Not even a vest?

Orit took me through the Old Town market in Jerusalem, and then through the winding side streets. Most of the shops were shut, closed in protest at Israeli police brutality in an incident the previous day. Occasionally she greeted an acquaintance, but we never stood still. Eventually the street widened out and we arrived at the Wailing Wall. The police were everywhere. A big man with an American accent was selling tefillin.

— Get yourself all strapped up for prayer!

Orit led me past the swaying bands of bearded, black clad Orthodox in big fur hats. She pointed:

— If you go through that gateway you will come to the Dome of the Rock, the Al Aqsa mosque, where Mohammed left the earth for heaven. I will wait here for you.

About an hour later I was back.

16

— *Well?*
— *It's beautiful.*
— *Did you go inside the mosque?*
— *No. They would not let me in.*
— *Why, because you are not a Moslem…*
— *No.*
— *Did you take off your shoes?*
— *Yes, I washed my feet in the fountain and I had my shoes in my hand, and I said I wanted to pray but the guy would not let me in. He said I was a tourist and should pay a fee.*
— *To a house of God? I don't understand.*
— *Well, he spoke pretty good English.*

We walked back to the Wailing Wall. Orit held out a pencil and a small square of paper.
— *You write your prayer, roll it up tight and insert it into a crack in the wall. I will leave you alone for a moment so you can think what you want to pray for. Afterwards she said:*
— *Can I ask what you prayed for?*
— *I don't pray. I wished. And no, you may not.*
— *Oh.*
— *It's private.*
— *OK… When you stood there touching the wall, did you feel anything?*
— *Such as?*
— *Some people say they feel a surge, ancient history, power, Jewishness… something, I don't know, flowing through them*
— *No. A rock. A nice warm rock…*
— *I don't think you will get what you wished for.*
— *Oh.*
— *I know what it was. And you won't get it.*
— *But…*
— *And if you did, you would not like it…*

When I got home Mrs Levertoff, the woman who has the flat upstairs from me, was just arriving home with her shopping.
— You must be exhausted from teaching all day, she said. Can I invite you in for coffee?
The first time I had met her, just after she had moved in, I invited her for coffee. She had declined my offer saying that she was Jewish and there were certain considerations she had to keep in mind.
— Oh. Keeping kosher? Well, you bring water from your own tap to my place, in a glass of your choosing. Bring a chaperone too, if you want. You don't have to do anything but breathe the air and drink the water. I just think it might be nice to talk… We are all humans, first and foremost.
— I will think about it, she said.

And she did. About an hour later there was a knock at my door. It was Mrs Levertoff.

— How about you come to me for coffee? she said.

— Best offer I've had all day.

We sat amid her packing case and boxes, sipping coffee. And after that she often invited me for what I came to call 'kosher coffee'.

— Tell me, she said the first time I visited, have you ever been to Israel?

— Yes, I have. Just for a few days last year.

— Where?

— All around. The Golan, Jerusalem, Aco, Ein Geddi, Massada, Haifa…

— And the Wailing Wall?

— Yes.

— And did you roll up a prayer and stick it into a crack?

— Well, no. I leaned on the wall and I wished very hard.

— And what was your impression?

— Of Israel? Sad. Everybody has stories about the war, the camps, missing family, terrible stories. I knew it would be like that…But some people think that gives them a kind of licence though, and it seemed to me there were, simply…well, a lot of nutcases looking for an excuse. And they were armed. It was very, very tense.

— You didn't like it?

— I loved the scenery, the climate. It was beautiful. Fantastic. But you can't live your life looking over your shoulder. At least I can't.

— But you are not involved, surely, you are out of it. A third party.

— Mrs Levertoff, if I go into a coffee shop and a nail bomb explodes, the nails don't suddenly swerve around me because I have an Irish passport. And if an Israeli tank comes busting through the walls of a house my liberal opinion will not turn it aside.

— This I cannot argue with. For myself, I was in Israel many, many times and I don't like it at all. I tried, God knows, but who could love such a place? Who could live with such people — unless, as you say, you are looking for trouble. What a mess! Brotherly love did not get us into this mess and it will not get us out. Now, tell me, when you were there, how was the food?

— Awful.

— You tried everything?

— Everything: even the pizza was poor. The Palestinian restaurants were only slightly better.

— On this I can agree.

— The ice cream was good…

— OK, sure, so the ice cream was good.

— And the olives, bread, humus…

— You are right. These people just don't know how to eat!

— Or drink.

— You mean the coffee?

— And the wine.

— And did you visit a kibbutz?

— Two.

— And there, the food was how?

— Even worse than everywhere else.

— Cream cheese?

— And gherkins.

18

— Ha! We agree.
— We do? That's good, Mrs Levertoff.
Mrs Levertoff and I parted on good terms that evening. She seemed entertained, even amused by me. I did not see her for a couple of days. The next time she invited me in she produced tiny little poppy-seed cakes and again we chatted for an hour or so. I was delighted to have a neighbour I could get on with – previous tenants in the upstairs flat had been unapproachable, a pair of 'professional skateboarders' and then some student nightmares. Mrs Levertoff and I, over several months, became good neighbours and, I think, good friends. I even gave her a key to my flat so that if I was away for a couple of days she could pop in and feed my cat.

Orit wanted me to see Israel.
— Perhaps you will never return, she said. So you should see as much as possible. We will make a kind of tour.

We drove through Tel Aviv on our way to Acre – Orit called it Aco. We drove slowly past large groups of Orthodox Jews in long black coats, some in long socks and gaiters, most in fur hats or wide brimmed black hats. All had long beards and side-locks. I was fascinated. Orit said:
— I bet you never see anything like this even in North Manchester.
— Like something from another age.
— Boruch called them Jewish cowboys.
— Very picturesque.
— Maybe. But if you try to drive through here on a Saturday, they will stone you. And I am not joking.

We ate in a restaurant that night. Orit was very quiet and hardly touched the food. Eventually she said:
— So when did you first become aware of Israel?
— From my uncle. I have photo of my uncle Mick standing outside the King David Hotel just before the war. He is in khaki shorts and carries a rifle slung over his shoulder. He is smiling, his eyes screwed up against the intense sunlight. He has three stripes on his arm, though he was in fact a corporal. That is because he is in the Irish Guards. Shortly after that he was called back to Britain, to prepare for the British Expeditionary Force to France. He fought at Boulogne. He was wounded and captured. He spent the next three years in a PoW camp in Germany before the Red Cross got him repatriated. He loved Palestine – Israel had not been invented then. He loved the climate. He could see that trouble was coming, but all the same he wanted to settle here. But it was not to be. His wounds called for several operations and for a long time after the war he needed special care before he could resume normal life. By the time he had recovered, well, Israel had been declared and it was no place for a one armed man… He stayed in Ireland, raised a family. After the war the Zionists bombed the King David hotel. I have seen pictures of the devastation. The path my uncle patrolled on his guard duty was under a mountain of rubble. I read that several of the Zionists who did this had served in the British Army. They intended to kill British Officers, but they killed a lot of Jews too.

Orit said:
— Did your uncle like the people here?
— Yes. He said: The Palestinians are the Jews of the Arab world.
Orit laughed:
— It's true. Nobody likes them… It is possible your uncle and my uncle fought each other. I wonder what Israelis would say now to this Irishman serving in the British Army. I wonder what an Irishman would say to them about Israel.
— Probably, as the Americans say, what goes around comes around.
— Yes. Maybe we could learn something from this.
— Let's hope somebody somewhere learns something from someone…
— If there is one thing we learn from history, it is that we do not learn from history.
— Who said that?
— Günter Grass. A German writer, who was also a Kashubian.
— A what?
— A kind of Pole.

This particular evening Mrs Levertoff put down her shopping and said:
— I moved here, she said, to be closer to my son, Isaac, you know, the highly successful dentist. His brother, Jacob, a lawyer, is married. But my Isaac has no luck in this direction and he is past his fortieth birthday. I have fixed him up a couple of times and even I got a marriage arranger to work on him. But nothing. So I think now he needs a little taking care of. And then, last week he rings me to say he has found a nice girl. The girl is called Alex. She was married before, but her husband drank a lot so she ran away from him when he beat her. She has a boy from that marriage. She lived in Blackpool. The boy is a bit uncared for I think. She is a dental nurse working for an agency. The agency sent her to work for my son the dentist as a temp. He brought her here on Friday night, so I met her. He is so totally in love with her. You should see how he looks at her. I never saw him like this before. I wish him to be married, so I say nothing.
— Sounds like the real thing.
— Yes. The real thing, maybe…
— Something troubling you, Mrs Levertoff?
— She says her grandparents were Jewish, but her mother 'married out', so she was not brought up in a Jewish home. Isaac is very serious. He knows her a week and already he proposed marriage. He says he will take on the son 'as part of the package'. Perhaps they will have other children. Isaac is head over heels. They are planning to holiday together and when they come back they will marry immediately. She seems to be a nice girl for my Isaac…but I will speak with Rabbi Hirsch…I must go. They are visiting me tonight and I want to make a cake.
   I had met Isaac a couple of times before. He had done some emergency dental work for me once, just after I moved to Manchester, but he would not take me on as an NHS patient and I could not afford his prices. He was large, boyish and generally affable, I thought. But I was curious to catch a glimpse of his new girlfriend, so that evening I made sure I was messing around in the front garden, pulling up weeds, filling in time, when Isaac and the girlfriend arrived. But tagging along behind them, I was surprised to see the boy and the dog who had been in my garden the other day. Isaac rang his mother's bell and while they waited to be let in he introduced me to Alex.

— I have already met your son and his dog, I said to her, and I explained what had happened.

— He never said anything to me, she said. But I am so sorry. They're a bit wild. Used to running around in the sand dunes at Blackpool, doing just as they please. Anyway, I hope you and the cat are OK.

She was very pretty, slightly flirty. I noticed high, wide cheek bones, wavy dark hair, blue eyes, a trim figure and long slim legs emphasised by the cotton summer skirt.

— Yes, I said. No real damage done.

I had the distinct impression that somehow she was sneering at me. Never mind me, I thought. You just catch your dentist.

We came to a small hill. Orit stopped the car. She pointed down the road in front of us.

— There. An Arab village. Whenever we came to an Arab village Boruch used to say: 'I see their rubbish dump, but where is their village?' It was not a good attitude, but sometimes I have to say he had a point. This car still has British licence plates. If we are lucky we will get through without a problem.

We drove on. The villagers stared at us, but nothing happened. Later, driving through Jericho, Arab kids stoned the car. A few chips in the windscreen and some scratches to the paintwork. No real damage. Neither of us was hurt.

We stopped overnight at a small red-roofed settlement and spent the night on inflatable mattresses in a concrete blockhouse. Next day we drove south, along the Dead Sea. We stopped at a beach front café. There were deck chairs beside a swimming pool. The pool was empty. The deck chairs were brittle and ragged. The faded canvas flapped in the breeze. The Dead Sea was about half a mile away. The café was closed up and deserted.

— Why did they build it here when the sea is over there?

— The sea was here when they built the place. But Israel and Jordan take so much water from the river the level of the sea has dropped. Neither side will agree to stop. They need the water for irrigation, for growing food. Soon the Dead Sea will just be this little mud puddle in a desert of sand and salt. But still, just enough to argue about.

We found a room for the night. The proprietor refused point blank to cook anything and there was no restaurant or café anywhere near, so we ate cream cheese and pickled gherkin sandwiches on the bed. We made love. After-wards Orit clung to me, tears on her face. I woke to find her looking at me very intently in the moonlight. She said:

– I don't want to waste my life. And that is what I am doing.

In the morning there was a breakfast of boiled eggs, fresh bread and lemon tea. Orit laughed:

– I think he feels a bit guilty about not feeding us last night.

We drove on to Masada {which Orit called Matsada} and spent the morning rambling over the great rock fortress, wondering at the underground cisterns, at the huge ramp the Romans had constructed to break into the fortress and at the fate of the final few defenders. Down below, at the base of the great rampart, we could see a group of archaeologists. We went down to see what they had found. They turned out to be French and it seemed they had found

among the rocks the broken bones of what they said might be the last few defenders of the fortress.
– They cut the throats of their loved ones and then jumped, said a young digger. They would not surrender and they would not be taken alive.
Late in the afternoon we drove on again. By the time we arrived at Ein Gedi we both had bright red faces from the wind and dust, and my normally straight hair had twisted and corkscrewed into a matted bush.

At break time Ariel, the Israeli student, took me aside to dish the dirt on the Palestinians. – You should see the mess they make everywhere. They are too busy making babies for Allah. You know they believe that if they become martyrs they will go to Paradise to reside with seventy virgins. They have sex on the brain. But this one – grey eyes and so pale. He doesn't look like an Arab. And why should he come here to study hydrology? There are plenty of places in Lebanon, Jordan, Syria, Egypt, even Palestine where he could study hydrology…Have you ever been to Israel? You should not judge it if you haven't seen it. I want to invite you. Come to my country. You will love it. You will see. You know the Irish have a bad history – almost as bad as ours. I meet the Irish scattered like Jews all over the world. Everywhere.

We sat out on the rocks at Ein Gedi, under the stars. Ten foot tall bamboo sighed in the night breeze. A rock hyrax snuffled and shuffled below us, clearly visible in the moonlight. Above us a few stars twinkled. I envied the hyrax his fur coat. I asked Orit what went wrong between her and Boruch. She thought for a moment and then said:
– I was married before, in America. He was orthodox. I had to cut off all my hair. It was not a good match. I was too young, too wild for him. I ran away. I came here. Got a flat in Tel Aviv – who could live in Jerusalem? I did my national service in the IDF and I met Boruch Cohen, a nice boy, I thought, son of a judge whose family came from Egypt in the 1950s. I thought maybe, with him, you know…But after we had been together for a couple of years and I said maybe we should think about getting married…At least talk about it. He said: 'I am a Kahane, descended from the judges and law givers of old, I cannot marry a divorced woman.' He said his family would never allow it. I went to his father and I asked if this was true. His father said it was true, they had a distinguished family history, but they wouldn't make any obstacle to our marriage. I asked his mother if there was a problem. She said no, they liked me. It was the boy. He did not want to marry me…After that, I just hung on as long as I could, hoping, you know…Right here, where we are sitting, is a natural spring. That's what the word ein means, a well or a spring. When the spring rains finish, this place will be about ten feet under water. You should see it then. Absolutely fantastic.
There was a long awkward silence. She said:
– Don't you think that what is happening here is a tragedy?
I was not sure where this was headed.
– A tragedy? I see a lot of bad behaviour, stupid stuff, posturing and provocation. I see two states trying to get born, where perhaps there should only be one: I see two peoples trying to get into the modern world when they would

move a lot easier if they marched in step. And I see two peoples clinging to his-
tory… Is that a tragedy? I don't know.
– One state? Are you crazy?
Next morning we turned around and headed north.
– When did you know it was over between you and Boruch?
– Really over? A long time ago. I thought I could make him change his mind, but
I just couldn't do it. Then one night we went into a bar in Tel Aviv and there was
this young guy with a big beard sitting there. He was from South Africa and he
and Boruch got talking and this man said: 'You know, Israel and South Africa
are in the same business.' 'What is that?' said Boruch. 'Controlling the fucking
kaffirs, man. It's the same war, I tell you.' And Boruch actually laughed. Then I
knew, I absolutely knew, I should get away from this man.

A few days later I met Mrs Levertoff again.
– How did the visit go? I asked. Do you like her a little bit now? Are they still in love?
Mrs Levertoff looked distressed.
– Come in, she said. I will tell you everything…
We went inside and she put on the kettle.
– I spoke with Rabbi Hirsch, said Mrs Levertoff. He knows a man. I asked that man and
he made certain inquiries. He found out that the girl had no real home. She was a den-
tal nurse, yes, but before she came here she lived in a caravan in Blackpool.
– Well, that's not so bad. It's not an offence…
– No home is not good. But the thing, the worst thing is that she is not Jewish at all.
She lied. Her mother did not 'marry out'. Her grandparents were not Jews.
– Oh, good grief.
– She said she will convert in order to marry my Isaac.
– What will Isaac do?
– She asks me the same question. I say, I leave that to Isaac. You will discuss this with him?
– I plan to, she said.
– I said: You better do more than plan missy.
– She says: If Isaac says OK?
– Then you will be my daughter-in-law.
– And that's that?
– That will be that.
– She says: It will be hard…
– I said: You want my Isaac, you must tell him.
– And did she, Mrs Levertoff?
– This is nearly killing him. My poor Isaac is heartbroken. He can't sleep. He can't eat.
He says she deceived him so she must go. The marriage is off.
– How could she hope to pull off such a stunt?
– The nerve of her! To do this to my boy!
– There is another boy involved.
– Her son. Ah…sure. My Isaac is one thing. From this she can walk away. But her
boy…from him she can't walk away.
– One minute he's running around with his dog on the beach at Blackpool, not a care
in the world. The next he's a Jew in Manchester, studying for his Bar Mitzva, and he's
gonna be circumcised.

We stopped the car on the top of a long slow rise.
– So are you saying the Jews should not be here?
– No. I'm saying the Palestinians were here when the Zionists arrived. They were not invisible. I am sure there must have been a better way to achieve things. Probably several better ways.
– Such as?
– Well, maybe attitude. Whether the Israelis like it or not the Palestinians are neighbours. Doesn't The Bible say: 'Love thy neighbour'?
– No. It says: 'Respect thy neighbour'.
– OK, but you are making my point for me. Let's say you live near me. If we have an argument, well, we had both better watch what we say and do because tomorrow we wake to find we still live next door to each other.
. – Are you judging us?
– I am an outsider. It's not for me to judge. I'm just saying what I see.
– Hmm…It's good you have your own opinion. You stand up for yourself. Do you know why I think this?
– No, I don't.
– Because I often meet people who talk total drivel about this place. They think I will not contradict them.
– Sounds complicated.
– Not very.
Orit pointed at the horizon.
– See. They are building the new security fence.
In the distance cranes and concrete mixers scurried about and a grey concrete worm advanced across the countryside, casting a long shadow.
– That's not a fence, I said. It's a wall, in fact it's a pale.
– Ah, like in Russia?
– We had one in Ireland. The Normans built it to keep the Irish out.
– And the Russians had one to keep the Jews in.
– My, how history repeats itself.
– You can take the Jew from the ghetto, but you cannot take the ghetto from the Jew.
– You are building your own ghetto this time.

When you teach English to overseas students, the women you meet tend to be foreign. I had a date that night, with a very attractive Tunisian divorcee called Fatimah, a former student of mine. Her father had a car import – export firm in Souss. In private she had taken off her headscarf and we had kissed, though in public we never so much as touched. This would be our third date. She said she had told her father about me and, as she put it: 'he did not die of a heart attack'. I had a suspicion that the question of whether I might convert to Islam would be up for discussion, probably over dinner. This would be Fatimah's way of finding out if I was prepared to consider marrying her. And if I knew Fatimah at all, she would reassure me I could always be a rather negligent Muslim.

Mrs Levertoff poured lemon tea and said:
– Tell me, when you were in Tel Aviv, did you walk along the sea front?

– I did.

– And what did you notice?

– Apart from the gunboat and the helicopter…?

– Apart from them.

– Well, there were only a few people on the beach. Very young people.

– And the place itself? The buildings?

– Modern, concrete, stylish, Bauhaus I think. But there was something odd…

– Yes?

– Yes. All the streets ran away from the beach. Very few properties had a view of the sea. I would have thought…well most people prize a sea-view.

– You are right. Do you know why?

– I have no idea.

– It is strange. Israelis claim to be a Middle Eastern people, but when they came to Israel, they did not know how to live there. They didn't pay any attention to the place, the climate, the scenery, they didn't recognise the local culture, the people – not even the food or the music. They didn't even dress right. The fact is mostly these people came from a shtetl or a ghetto in Eastern Europe. They dreamed of Warsaw or Minsk. And that was what they tried to recreate. And they didn't mean to, but I think they took with them a European attitude of superiority, a kind of colonialist mentality. The people already there, they were just Arabs, they didn't count … That reminds me, how are you getting on with your students – the Israeli and the Palestinian?

– They are driving me nuts. But if you can get them off the topic of each other, they are both nice enough. The forces that made them stretch into the past: and their worlds are shaped by people who perpetuate those events and identities – either victims of it or the people who profit from it, people who have something to loose. Neither seems able to step back to see who they really are. They are just history in action.

Orit had a friend called Tali. They had served together in the Israeli Defence Force. Tali had married a settler called Avshalom and they had three children and a small farm on the Golan Heights.

– She has had the reverse experience to mine. In every way, said Orit, she has become orthodox. She is not the wild young woman I knew, but the respectable wife of a devout Jew and staunch Israeli. She has a wig made of her own hair and they think of nothing else but making babies and turning Israel into a religious state.

I took this as a warning. The Golan was green, wet and cold. On the twisting mountain road we passed several burned out Russian-made tanks, rusting quietly in the rain.

– There was heavy fighting here. Orit explained. Many Israelis died to take this place.

Tali and Orit greeted each other like long-lost sisters. Avshalom was polite but distant. Their concrete home had a red-tile roof, but otherwise was like a military bunker with steel shutters over the doors and slit windows. There were weapons – assault rifles, pistols – in a rack behind the door. Over dinner, which was the first real food Orit and I had eaten in four days, Orit translated my questions. How long have you been here, what do you grow, where do the children go to school. The usual. After dinner Avshalom took us round the property.

– If Israel trades the Golan with Syria in return for a guarantee of peace, what will Tali and Avshalom do?

Avshalom snarled.

– He says they will fight anyone who tries to take this land from them – Israeli or Syrian.

– Yeah, I think in the Bible Joshua started that – you know, when the Jews arrived here they had to fight the locals. The siege of Jericho. Even then, although it was the Promised Land, somehow God never quite delivered on the promise. And then Israel never quite recovered from the war of 1967.

– But we won that war.

– I know. And since then diplomacy never had a chance.

She translated for Avshalom. He bent down and scooped up a handful of dirt and grass.

– He says this is Israeli soil, whatever the government thinks.

– Dirt has a passport now? How can I tell Israeli dirt from Syrian dirt?

– He says: God gave us this land. It was promised.

– Is it possible to promise something that is not yours?

– He says it was a binding promise from God.

– That would not stand up in a court of law, even here: where is the legal document?

– The Bible, he says.

– Is it signed? Witnessed? Where are the original deeds? Other people think they own the land…

– You speak like a lawyer. Please, we are guests in his house. Don't make him angry.

I shrugged.

– We are just discussing… Everybody's got to be somewhere, right? And he's in a bad mood anyway. Why is that?

– His neighbour had a calf. An unspotted red calf. But it died last night.

– I don't get it…

– It was a prophesy. The sacrifice of a perfect, unblemished red calf signifies the Third Temple, the coming of the Messiah, the end of days.

– Oh…

Avshalom was looking around nervously.

– We should go inside now.

By the barn Orit and Avshalom paused, exchanged a few more words, then we headed indoors. That night Orit said:.

– Avshalom is a bit scary, no?

– He is. I suppose a lot of Israelis think like him. What were you talking about, just before we came in?

– Nothing.

– I heard my name.

Orit sat back and folded her arms.

– He wanted to know if you will convert when we marry.

– What did you say?

– I said you won't convert, you have enough problems already. Also I said we won't marry. It is not like that between us.

27

– Oh…
She kissed me.
– Silly boy. I said you would not get your wish.

It was to my considerable relief that the English summer course came to an end. I helped organise a party before the group split up, but separately both Ariel and Javid excused themselves saying they found the European students' consumption of alcohol a problem. I heard later that they had both gone to see a film called *The Syrian Wife* at the Cornerhouse, and had encountered each other there. It was the first time they had met outside the classroom. Apparently they were polite but wary. Nevertheless they sat next to each other through the film and afterwards they went for coffee, had a serious discussion and even exchanged addresses. I never saw them again. They had both invited me to 'their country', but neither of them left me an address.

That evening I was weary at having to complete so many student course reports, but Mrs Levertoff insisted I eat strudel with her. She was in fine form and the strudel was delicious. She seemed to have recovered from the shock about Alex, who had not returned to the dentist's surgery to work, and according to the agency, had disappeared.
– So how was the date?
– With Fatimah?
– Yes, the nice Arab girl.
– It was good. Fine.
– Good, I like. But good followed by fine?
– I have been out with Muslim girls before. Things never get beyond the third date.
– I see.

Our last stop was to visit Orit's aunt Ida. She lived on a Kibbutz in the Galilee or Kineret, as Orit called it. Ida took us to the canteen, but it was closing and there was only cold tea, cream cheese and gherkins. We piled up our plates and ate without enthusiasm in silence. There seemed to be some tension between Orit and her aunt. Ida did not seem at all curious about me. She spoke directly to me only once:
– So, you're not Jewish?
– No.
– From England?
– I live in England…
– I see.
I was not sure what she saw.
In the morning we were up at first light to get breakfast, while there was still some breakfast to get. I don't know what I expected, but even though we were among the first, tea, bread, cream cheese and gherkins was all we could find. Orit said:
– It wasn't always like this. When Boruch and I were on a kibbutz we all ate together and nobody had private property. We spent all day making sprinklers for the field system or tending turkeys. It was hard. Most people could not live like that for long, so they changed the rules. Now they can eat in their own

place, and the kitchens provide only a few things. It's not so good.
– How long has your aunt been here?
– More than twenty years. She came from America. At first she lived with my mother in Tel Aviv, but they quarrelled. She came here. They haven't spoken since. It is important that you know, here in Israel we all hate everybody...And everybody hates the Yeckers.
– The Yeckers?
– The German Jews.
It was full light by now and we watched a horde of cyclists heading out through the main gate towards the fields and fruit groves.
– You see, they have baskets on the front of their bikes, like delivery boys?
– Yes.
– The more important you are the bigger your basket... That's a kibbutz joke.

That night I dreamt that they put me in charge of making peace. We met at a big hole in the new security wall. All the big names were there. Ariel Sharon came up to me and I said to him:
– Why aren't you doing this?
He smiled and said:
– We can't put a killer in charge of making peace, can we?
In my dream I had money, foreign money, cash, for both sides, if only they would stop what they were doing. I said:
– You can have the money, but you can't buy weapons with it. Do you agree?
They all nodded in agreement. The Arabs bought new donkeys and the Israelis all got new bathrooms. Don't ask me why. And then we knocked an even bigger hole in the wall and while the Israeli men set off up a long trench towards the shops smoking and arguing about the various bathrooms you could get, the Arab men all stood around smoking, spitting and admiring their new donkeys. The Arab women, however, scrambled through the hole in the wall and admired the Israeli babies and then the Israeli women climbed back through the wall dragging their prams and they pushed the Arab babies around in the prams in a great big circle while they sang lullabies. How did they get the prams through the hole in the wall? I have no idea – it was a dream. I told all this to Orit. She listened and then said:
– Where did that come from?
– I don't know, but I don't think it was my dream...
– What?
– It was like I intercepted someone else's dream.
– Your dreams are weird.
– Yeah, I said. A dream of peace. How weird is that?
– You know, I think you are slightly mad.

– So. But now I have an idea...said Mrs Levertoff.
– Tell me...
– You know I am certain I could find a nice Jewish girl for you in a couple of weeks.
– Ah, but, then I would have to convert...
– You are worried about the observances, the children, what? Relax, you don't have

to be a good Jew…So many nice Jewish girls…If I were a few years younger I would undertake to convince you myself. And from this, believe me, you would not resist. You look at me now and you see an old lady, yes? But if you met me when I was a young woman it would be different story. Look!

She plucked a photograph from a pile on the sideboard and handed it to me.

– Mrs Levertoff, this is you?

– You betcha is me. I had my life. But you, I reckon you are a couple of years younger then my Isaac. So what you say, I fix up something? A few accidental encounters, maybe. And if you see somebody you like, you tell me and we see …

– And the Jewish thing?

– The Jewish thing? Well we leave it somewhere in the background. Then we see later, maybe. Yes? We are human beings first.

Orit took me to Tel Aviv airport. The palm trees whipped about in the breeze. She hugged me long and kissed me hard.

– It was great.

– It was.

– I had a good time.

– Me too.

– Take care of yourself.

– You too.

– Will you write?

– Mm…I don't think so.

Her mouth was smiling, but her eyes were cool and hard and very blue.

As usual the security check was long and thorough. They searched my bags, searched me, double-checked the provenance of my ticket and shone a light up my passport's arse. The security man said:

– Did you travel in Israel?

– Yes.

– Where?

– All over.

– What do you think?

– A beautiful mess.

– So what was your business in Israel?

– A girl.

– An Israeli?

– Yes.

– Very probably it won't work out, I'm sorry to say.

He sighed, handed me my passport

– You're through, he said and waved his hand.

– I know, I said.

Carl Tighe is the author of several works of both fiction and non-fiction. His novel *Druids Hill* (no apostrophe) was published by Five Leaves in 2009. He is working on a new novel and (as always) looking for an agent.

Robert Sward

The Astronomer, A Universe for Beginners

1. The Astronomer

MATH TEACHER: Sexual position when you are doing your partner and you
yell out math problems like "What is the square root of 4?" and "What is 5+5?"
You fuck him/her harder and harder to try to get these simple problems wrong.
— Urban Dictionary

Celeste:
"All galaxies in observable space
Recede from ours at the speed of light."
I follow, undergrad taking notes.
I'm with her, the astronomer.
"What's the square root of four?" she asks
            all aglow,
Straddling me in the morning light. I'm imagining…
            milky white and pinkish blue…
"Continuous creation out of nothing from nowhere."
She looks around the lecture hall. Points at me.
"What are we here for?"
"*I dunno,*" I say, flustered. "*I mean…*"
"In the beginning there was nowhere," she says.
"It all began with a ball of gas vibrating
And a great roaring," I scribble.
"The entire observable universe
            would have been
                        about the size of a grain of sand."
Jesus, I'm thinking, now that's the way to begin a story!

But there's a complication.
"Our universe should be slowing down," she says,
"Instead, it's speeding up…
And galaxies are being forced further and further apart,
Stretching the very fabric of space."
Now she's riding me, harder, harder…
"The energy for that has to come from somewhere.
Dark, we call it, dark as in 'unknown,' dark…the dark forever."
O…Celeste, O Celeste!

2. Dark Matter

COLLAPSING THE DECKCHAIR: Sexual position in which the receiver lays [sic] on his/her back, with waist at the edge of a bed. The giver stands next to the bed, with the receiver's legs on his/her shoulders. While penetrating, the giver may – at his/her discretion – lean forward to create extra tension.
— Urban Dictionary

Celeste:
Teacher with a giant star chart, the whole of heaven in her arms.
"You'll need a telescope." Adjusts her Orion SyQuest…
"Can you see it?" Points – to…
On my knees, squinting, I bow before the eyepiece.
"Cassiopeia," she announces, "the Seated Queen…
Cassiopeia in a deck chair."
"Up periscope! Go Bronco Buster," I'm thinking,
"Missionary Position, Side Entry Constellation,
Puppet Master…"
"Legs up, legs up," I hear her say. "R U ready?"
What? What'd she say?
C student, I can barely keep up, don't know the math.
It's all darkness, a Universe for Beginners.
"Cassiopeia is at the edge of the Milky Way," she goes on.
"Five bright stars in the constellation form a rough 'W' in the sky. Some see this
    formation in the shape of a chair.
"You over there, Mr Sward" – gestures from her lectern –
    "name and locate four others."
"Swing Time, Lazy Man, Belly Flop, Man Chair…" I say.
Digs in her heels beside her hips. I'm imagining…
"Align yourself," says Celeste. "Consider the angle –
That's it, that's it," *Figure 8 Swivel,*
The Lock and Pose, the Space Wheel…
"The bulk of matter in the universe is dark," she says.
"It's the invisible scaffolding for the formation of stars."
"Dark matter," she goes on, "dark matter exerts a ghostly pull
On normal matter…"
Her ankles round my neck, I kiss her knees,
Leaning now, leaning forward
O…Celeste, Celesta, Ce-les-tas, Ce-leste.

3. Space Wheel

SPACE WHEEL: Sexual position that can only be performed effectively in outer space and less effectively while submerged underwater. The position is characterized by a standing doggy style without thrusting but rather with a circular motion of the female participant just like an airplane propeller.
– Urban Dictionary

Celeste:
"Mass can consist of both visible matter, like stars,
And invisible dark matter," she says.
"Dark matter: a web-like structure...
Stretches throughout space," I scribble.
"Only because of the hidden,
     does the visible world exist," she goes on.
What...whaat? I've lost her.
"Let me explain. Most of the universe seems to consist of nothing we can see.
4 % visible matter; 96 % invisible...
And imagine: Dark energy makes up over 2/3 of the energy
In the universe, dark energy, some say,
That's what's pushing the universe apart." She holds up a chart.

We huddle together at the bottom of a pool,
Beanpole undergrad and the astronomer,
Clerestory windows above us. Imagining...
"You know, there's no escape," she says.
"Gravity, *gravity* holds it all together,"
"There is a way," I say, grasping her from behind,
As, weightless, *near* weightless,
     she begins to rotate,
     spinning
Faster and faster
Tight, black neoprene silver goggles and angel fins
Celeste, O Celeste, spiraling
Kissing first her neck, then her ankles, neck, ankles,
Auburn hair afloat and whirls
As still she turns, propeller, O propeller
And we rise heavenward from the tiled bottom
Beanpole and mermaid professor
Dawn's early light, rockets' red glare
Lecture hall and telescopes lectern spinning in air
O Celeste, Celeste,
          O fairest of the fair!

Robert Sward has taught at Cornell University, the Iowa Writers' Workshop and UC Santa Cruz. He has been a contributor to *Ambit* since the mid-1960s and is the author of *Heavenly Sex*, *The Collected Poems* and the forthcoming *New and Selected 1957–2011*.

Judy Brown

The Helicopter Pilot's Lament

You'd never believe how easy it is
to lose your way – how our bearings slur
as we cross the city in under ten minutes,
tracing the unbuilt spaces where London splits to green.
How the dawn breaks open, orange and fatal,
like a pomegranate landing on concrete.

Or how our instruments see too much
I sometimes think – from the itch of the chestnut candles
starting to fire to tigerworms threading
the compost heaps with red. And down there:
that pair of pale trousers prone on the decking,
rained-on and stained with chianti.

But I've come to crave exactly this –
the taste of the morning before it's tainted,
I'm the man who watches rush hour build
like silver coral. I crack the codes – the dots
and checks on squad cars – or track
the mercy dash of an ambulance.

All too soon we hang overhead, a thudding
barge of air, settle our weight into the slack,
the landing space. It's weird, even now,
how the crowded colours of earth stripe the glass
as we're suddenly sucked down. We spill –
friction hot – into the morning at Willesden.

The ground seems to bruise my feet
as I head for my cooling bed where only
a lukewarm dent remains of a dayshift girlfriend.
And above me the gods are strung
like fine chandeliers and I admit to myself
again and again: *I do not want to be home*.

Judy Brown's pamphlet, *Pillars of Salt* (2006), was a winner in Templar Poetry's
pamphlet competition. She won the Poetry London competition in 2009 and in
2005 received the Poetry Society's Hamish Canham Poetry Prize. Her first
collection is forthcoming from Seren in 2011.

Robin Helweg-Larsen

This Ape I Am

Under our armoured mirrors of the mind
Where eyes watch eyes, trying to pierce disguise,
An ape, incapable of doubt, looks out,
Insists this world he sees is trees, and tries
To find the scenes his genes have predefined.

This ape I am
Who counts 'One, two, more, more'
Has lived three million years in empty lands
Where all the members of the roving bands
He's ever met have totalled some ten score;
So all these hundred thousands in the street
With voided eyes and quick avoiding feet
Must be the mere two hundred known before.

This ape I am
Believes they know me too.
I'm free to stare, smile, challenge, talk to you.

This ape I am
Thinks every female mine,
At least as much as any other male's;
If she's with someone else, she can defect –
Her choice, and she becomes mine to protect;
Just as each child must be kept safe and hale
For no one knows but that it could be mine.

This ape I am
Feels drugged, ecstatic, doped,
Hallucination-torn, kaleidoscoped,
That Earth's two hundred people includes swirls
Of limitless and ever-varied girls.

This ape I am
Does not look at myself
Doesn't know about mirrors, lack of health,
Doesn't know fear of death, only of cold;
Mirrorless, can't be ugly, can't be old.

English Businessman on a Park Bench

'I like this park bench – see the solid arm?
So if I fall asleep, me head won't freeze,
Me going bald and all, when there's a breeze;
I like a quick kip when the sun's this warm.'

Doves coo – a fountain plays – sky holds a kite –
The air's narcissus-sweet – the flag poles clack;
The slats are hard under his hips and back,
His jacket's underneath his head; tie's tight.

'I'll do a million this year – I'm no giant;
Sell out for three times that, with skill and luck –
Split with the wife, of course – regret the sale –
You always wish you had just one more client!
And ask the eternal question of the male:
Where do I find hot girls who want to fuck?'

Never Believe

Never believe the lies of war, and the orders
That seem to make sense –
Whether Hitler or Bush, no one storms over borders
'In self defence'.

'Leading the Free World' by having the biggest gun
Has always chilled
Those on whom the guns are turned, on everyone
Free to be killed.

Many Ways to Drown

America gives many ways to drown:
Unsupervised motel pools trap stray tots
Who can't reverse their tiptoe down the slope;
Kids who can swim explore the same pool's drain,
Get suctioned to it, have their guts ripped out;
Teens play in creeks in flood, or riptide beach;
A flooding river sweeps cars off the road;
New Orleans' levees break and thousands die.
For all of these, poor government shares blame –
Loose laws, weak education, lack of funds,
All driven by those tax breaks for the rich.
(Oh – add rendition's waterboarding deaths.)
But I drown in girls' large-eyed innocence,
Pools of enchantment and primordial depth.

Robin is an ape who is fascinated by the
apeness of sex, violence, ageing and death.

David Remfry

New York Tattoos

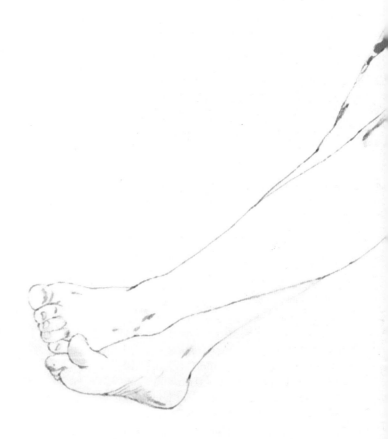

Judith Kazantzis

In the Suburb of the Bronze Doors

(extract, part 1 of 3)

Time clickety clicks through the fog
and we learn again to scrub these dull scenes

of expulsion, suffering, redemption
to their pitch perfect factory shine.

The last click comes! Ditching the polish,
we behold Sesame. Lo,

the dazzling doors,
like a lion's mouth at a beetle.

See them split wide, and Adam and Eve
& Pinchme, or just me,

we'll walk from the pensive allotment
where we dug an ash garden

for all these ash years, returning at night
to the ash hotel room.

Slowly to Bed

Slowly to bed, never to rise,
After her death, after she died –
miles and miles back to her smile,
a diamond ring for growing older,
a gold leaf for growing wiser.

All the world on her doorstep,
leaf pirouettes from the tulip tree,
shall I have it, you will snatch it,
hide it in your glittery pocket,
old forever and last week.

In a wallet we display
grit and bone bits on the shelf,
and what a muddle in all her rooms.
By turns I'm thin as a broom, then gold,
I die underground, and bloom,

a bloom without a stem for help,
without a twig or branch for help
and never a tree for help
and need no leaf nor tree for help
and never a tree nor leaf for help.

Salt Lick

I licked it up and kept it in,
closed my lips and sank my chin.
She lives away, in heaven or hell,
the one who never loved me well.
She must have lived because she's dead.
Jam and butter and a pinch of bread.
Old salt scar on old white skin,
such bitterness will do you in.
A drip of milk ran down my chin,
I licked it up and tucked it in.

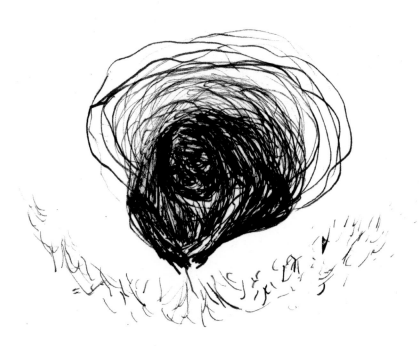

Ambit has published Judith Kazantzis' poetry and occasional fiction since the 1970s. In 2007 she received the Society of Authors' Cholmondeley Award for poetic achievement. Her next book is *Sister Invention* (2011). For more information go to www.judithkazantzis.com.

Florence Elon

Locked In

Along the hall, he skates,
crying, 'I'm not myself.'
Halts in front of a closet,
pulls out slacks and shirts,
'This is my agenda,
I'm being hunted.'
Slips into the bathroom,
slamming the door behind him,
bangs with fists: tight shut.

You're outside, he's inside –
that's the situation.
You squat on the hall floor;
sit and cross your legs,
folding your arms,
like some decorative doorstop
in the shape of a Buddha.
What's there to do
but wait it out, assume
a meditative posture?

Now numb, in shock, begin
remembering
how you were told to handle
things if your partner starts
unravelling –
hold still (your head a spool
of tangled wool) – unwind,
untwist, rewind.

Missing Person

Open our door: a silver badge dances
in the noon sun, straight teeth gleam
as he informs me *These people –*
especially those mental escapees –
often hide near their own houses.
He wants to have a look around.

Dumbly, I nod. My robot legs
follow this policeman
down our driveway to the never-locked
garage, our kids' haven.
He lifts torn blankets on an old sofa
but finds no sleeper-embryo
or jack-in-the-box crouched under
the ping-pong table, ready to jump.

Come out, come out wherever you are
I'm chanting silently, a child again,
wanting you back where you were,
and this to be our game.

Blue sleeves open the basement closet
that contains no body
inhabiting your coat, shirts in boxes
marked for the Salvation Army.

Lady, there are only a certain number
of places where those people go
in the environs of their homes.
Show me – *you gotta know.*

Where would you (or I) hide?
Against a wall, dark as a fly?
Behind long drapes, which one? Lying
in the bathtub: empty – or full?

I lead him to our garden shed
that shields some seeds, the tools,
half-expecting you to shoot up
among those hibernating bulbs,
cats napping, spiders and their webs,
dark squashed knots clogging screens.

Florence Elon's poems have been published by Chatto, Secker, several smaller
presses, anthologies, and many journals.

Noel Monahan

Scarecrow Woman

I catch sight of her on a sea of wheat
Drifting past, her blouse, jumper and skirt
Clamped to her bones with clothes-pegs,
Her face veiled in old straining-cloth,
A Sunday hat one side of her head
Alone in the field with her secrets,
A black diamond stitched to her sleeve
To remind us of winter and her dead daughter.
Perched on a wooden leg on golden grain,
She sways to scare the crows away,
Drinks rain, breathes the wind,
A sprinkle of poppies ignites the ripples,
Her promise always, the gift of grain
And the hope of tomorrow.

Gathering Mushrooms

We climbed into Tully's field, the gate rattled,
Sheep scattered, cows stood their ground as we strolled
Around in the hope of finding mushrooms.
You're blind as bats, Madge Reilly said,
I can see them sleeping under bedstraw
Hear them whispering in their dreams,
Her black thumb quenching the stars in the grass,
Their frail pink gills breathing a final tune.
Nightfall, the road lit up with sparks
Of mushrooms beaming from bucket and hand,
Like pilgrims returning from the Holy Land,
Thraneens laden, beads dangling in the dark,
A glimmer from lost fields I long to find
Hidden somewhere in the back of my mind.

Note: Thraneens is a Hiberno-English word meaning a long wisp of grass.

Noel Monahan has four books of poetry published by Salmon Poetry: *Opposite Walls* (1991), *Snowfire* (1995), *Curse Of The Birds* (2000) and *The Funeral Game* (2004). He has won several awards for his writing including: Poetry Ireland Seacat National Award, RTE P. J. O'Connor Drama Award and The Irish Writers Union Award for Poetry. His fifth collection of poetry will be published by Salmon Poetry in 2010.

Shining a Light

Deborah Levy

Alice is waiting in baggage reclaim at Prague airport and knows (before it is completely certain) that her bag will not appear. It has been lost. The cheerfully alienated official in charge of missing luggage (her name is Petra) knows this too.

Petra understands that filling in the form is a waste of both their time but Alice forces her shaking left hand to grip the chewed-up biro and describe her self as some one who has lost everything. Petra's breath smells of aniseed or something like that. Alice isn't really bothering, she can barely read her own hurried writing. The worst thing is that her mobile phone charger is in the bag that has gone missing. Even if the airline does find it somewhere and calls her to collect it, calls her to reclaim all that has been lost, her phone will be out of charge.

It is the last Saturday in August. Alice is dancing in the blue dress she has worn for three days while she watches an outdoor screening of Martin Scorsese's film of the Rolling Stones in concert. She is in a park in central Prague, midges are biting her arms, it is eleven at night and the moon is shining on the crowd. Two Serbian women, Jasna and Adrijana, are dancing with her while Mick Jagger sings 'Yeah You Light Up My Life'. When he walks away from the microphone to change his costume, Alice tells Jasna the stage goes dead when he is not on it. Like the luggage belt at the airport when she realised her bag was not there.

Jasna and Adrijana's boyfriends are queueing for beers. They wave to a man selling frankfurters so their girlfriends can buy hot dogs. Adrijana insists on getting one for Alice too, even though they have just met. They all smother the hotdogs in ketchup and drink beer and watch six swans sleeping on the black water of the Vlatva. Adrijana invites Alice to join them all for a swim the next day in a lake just outside Prague. Apparently it's not really a lake, it's an old mine that flooded a few years ago in a rainstorm. It is near a corn field, and there are castles and woods and eagles. Later, when Alice walks drunkenly over the cobblestones towards her hotel in Mala Strana she realises that arriving in a country with nothing but the clothes she is wearing has made her feel braver. Braver but freaked out.

The car that pulls up outside her hotel on Sunday afternoon is a beaten-up Mercedes. Adrijana shares the Merc with three other families and Sunday is her driving day. Jasna, Petar and Dimitar who are sitting in the back, move up to make room for Alice to squeeze in. There is someone else in the car too. He is introduced to Alice as a famous brilliant terrific genius composer of electronic music. The composer tells her his name is Alex but she can call him Mr Composer if she likes. And then he doesn't say a word for the entire journey.

When they finally arrive at the lake that had once been a mine, the green water is still and flat. Alice thinks it might have some sort of force that will suck her deep into the earth and make her disappear like her lost suitcase. Jasna lends her a swimming costume but Alice takes her time getting changed. Everyone is in the water, except for Mr Composer who refuses to swim and sits shivering on a rock buttoning up his jacket. When he catches Alice's eye he shrugs his shoulders and wryly translates the

Charles Shearer

sign at the entrance to the lake. He says it says DANGER! NO SWIMMING! He watches her climb down the clay path and dive into the water. It is very cold and she cannot feel her legs. Adrijana and Jasna have swum out to the centre of the lake where it is deepest and coldest. They have pinned up their brown hair and swim calmly and slowly together like the swans on the Vlatva.

Alice climbs out of the water and sits dripping wet next to Mr Composer or Alex or whoever he is. He hands her a plastic carrier bag. Inside it is a heavy square of cake. He explains that it is baklava made by his mother who he has just returned from visiting in Belgrade. It it is not like the baklava Alice is used to because it's heavy like bread. Please thank your mother for me, Alice says. He takes out his mobile and Alice hears him say, I'm at a lake outside Prague with Alice who is from Britain. She wants me to tell you she likes your cake.

When he ends the call Alice points out he has the same mobile phone as she does. That's really interesting Alice, he says, and tells her that he, like Adrijana and Jasna, had to cross three borders 'during the war' to get to Prague. Every now and again she notices a strained look in his eyes. She is just about to ask him something when Jasna creeps up behind her holding her blue dress.

On the way back to Prague they stop at a pub for beer and Alex orders a plate of smoked ham. While the others are talking he tells Alice that though they are all from Serbia they did not know each other in their own country. In fact, he says, we didn't really want to meet each other at first because you never know what each other is going to be like. Adrijana asks Alice if she has heard of a famous male philosopher from their country? She tells her the philosopher's name.

No, I've never heard of him, Alice sips her beer. Well he has this beautiful wife Adrijana says to Alice. Beautiful like you. Long blonde hair. But this philosopher who we like very much because he is always laughing like us, is also very busy. Very very busy. Always giving papers and lectures all over the world. In fact right now he is probably writing a lecture somewhere and it is midnight and the philosopher's beau-tiful wife is on the phone and she is saying to her husband, so kiss yourself good night tonight and I will kiss myself good night and you stroke your own hair tonight and I will stroke my own arm tonight. Alice does not really understand why they are all laughing so much until Adrijana explains the philosopher was born in the country they are from. Alice wants to tell her new friends about how her suitcase got lost at the airport but stops herself because although they are laughing they look freaked out.

Are you okay Alice? Alex prods her arm with his long fingers. By the way, he says, I really like your blue dress. He asks her when she is returning to the UK? She tells him she is leaving later that evening. Uh huh he says. Then tonight you will kiss your self good night. And I will kiss myself goodnight. He tells her he's going for a walk in the woods to stretch his legs before the drive back to Prague. The woods are just across the road from the pub. Alice asks if he minds if she joins him? She wants to see autumn leaves…

The sky has clouded by the time Alex and Alice cross the road to where the entrance to the woods begins. When they get there Alice doesn't want to walk with him after all. If she walks in to the woods she might come back changed into some-thing else. If she walks into the woods it will be like walking into herself where it is dark and trees bleed when cut with an axe.

She says, well, anyway, I'm really happy to meet you. He waves his hands around a bit and suddenly grabs the ends of her blonde hair with his fingertips. She wants to ask him about his music and where on the map the Balkans are, but she doesn't know where to begin. He lets go of her hair and he says, I really like so much your blue dress and red tights. If I stop working in my stupid job, one day I will buy you a pair of shoes. And then he walks into the woods.

She is waiting for Alex to come out of the woods. The season is turning and she wants to go home to England. A bird scrambles in the upper branches of a tree she cannot name. In England she can name all the trees. She watches the bird and she thinks about Adrijana and Jasna swimming in the deep cold lake. They have seen things she cannot imagine. They have been hurt in ways she has not been hurt. They have left all the seasons in their country behind them.

When she looks at her watch she wonders if Alex might have got lost. Has something happened to him in the wood? She bites the ends of her hair. This is how she felt at baggage reclaim. A feeling of dread in her stomach when she knew her bag had gone missing. Strange thoughts occur to her now as she waits for him. She thinks things she doesn't want to think about. She thinks there are people hiding in the woods because they have lost their homes and their children and their sisters and mothers and she thinks Alex might have lost his brother and father and she thinks she hears a gun going off and the rustle of leaves and birds crying out. She wants him to come back more than she ever wanted her luggage to come back. She is trembling and hugging her ribs and the material of her blue dress is rubbing against her skin as she paces up and down the road on the edge of the woods. A wind suddenly blows in and then she sees him.

He is walking towards her. There are small leaves in his hair as he stands too close and tells her his name is not Alex. Not exactly. It is Aleksandar. He tells her he wanted to kiss her in the woods and he is sorry to have missed the Rolling Stones film last night in the park because then he would have been near her a little bit longer. Does she know that Martin Scorsese wanted to be a priest before he became a film director?

Aleksandar squeezes his lips and lowers his eyes. He offers to charge up her mobile phone for her before she leaves for London. He folds his arms across his chest and leans back on his heels as if to get a better view of her and then he tells her it's nice to watch her laughing at him while the wind blows her hair about.

'Shining a Light' was first written for the 'Turning of the Seasons Project' at the Wapping Art Space, directed by Jules Wright.

Deborah Levy's novels include *Beautiful Mutants*, *Swallowing Geography*, *The Unloved* (Vintage), *Billy and Girl* (Bloomsbury/Dalkey Archives USA). An extract from her forthcoming novel 'Swimming Home' is extracted in Best European Fiction 2010 (Dalkey Archive). www.deborahlevy.co.uk.

Richard Gwyn

No Love for the Enemy

I ate cold stew and wondered how long it would be before the night sea crossing. They had been preparing small fishing launches and cruisers, trawlers and cargo ships, every manner of vessel, but still the departure was delayed by inclement weather. I lay concealed behind a gorse bush on the heights above the harbour, peering down through Russian binoculars. I was not certain who I was spying for. The enemy had attempted to recruit me and I had acceded to their request in order to prevent them killing me. But I had no love for the enemy. My own tribe was a disgrace, commandeering vegetable plots and chickens, putting psychotropics in the drinking water, confiscating all the mannequins from the major department stores and lining them, in army uniform, along the clifftops. As if anyone would be fooled by that! There was a third allegiance I was considering, the side which had supplied me with these fine binoculars and a warm leather jacket that made me feel like a god. It was this that tilted the balance, I think. That evening, after my day's vigil in the gorse-bush, I visited the local pub. Young women clung to me (or to my jacket) as if I were a screen idol. I pleasured one of them in a shed behind the tavern car-park. This is the life, I thought, slinging my binoculars around my neck and setting off through the night.

More of Everything

Alice remembers standing next to a stolen Mercedes on a mountain road in Spain. She was with Luc, a thief and trafficker of marijuana. They were waiting for nightfall before crossing into France along a smuggler track through the Pyrenees. She was smoking the merchandise and staring over the hills that fell away to the sea. Her life had changed considerably. She ate in quality restaurants and dressed in silks. She no longer worked the vendange or hung out with the winos in Plaza de la Trinidad. The bonnet of the big car was still warm and she lay back on it. Luc emerged from the car, and placed his hand between her legs. She closed her eyes. When night seeped into the valley, they prepared to leave. Alice sat up on the bonnet and saw a wild boar, a sow, trotting down the track towards them, followed by two young. She was delighted, signalled Luc to be still. The large boar stopped at twenty paces from the car, sniffed the air, then turned and stared at Alice. The two young boar stopped in synchrony, transfixed. Then, with a snort and a squeal and a scraping of hooves on the dust road, the three set off at a gallop through the gorse. Alice marvelled at the strength and purpose in the sow's movement as she charged along the hillside, white tusks brushing the low grass. Alice slid off the bonnet and into the car. Watching the animals run had made her want more of everything.

Richard Gwyn is a poet and novelist, whose website can be found at www.richardgwyn.com. His latest collection of prose poems, *Sad Giraffe Café*, is published by Arc.

Edmund Prestwich

Egyptian Labourers

Naked under the sun,
patient as earth itself, these men,
inheritors of nothing, worked
with sickles of flint teeth
to cut their master's corn.

Better the work of the fishponds, wading
among cool fish, though bitten by leeches,
their eyes hurt by splintering light;
worse the quarries, digging stone
with hoes of wood or picks of bone,
breaking up stone with stone.

Humble, soon forgotten,
like earthworms ploughing earth,
like insects labouring,
they lifted pyramids to the stars,
then walked away and left them to dead kings.

Hindu Goddesses

Crowded on these walls
fortune's gifts and nature's bounty,
sacred pools and trees and rivers,
love and treasure,

offer joy to men
in the forms of lithe, caressing
sculptured girls with yearning faces,
lips protruded,

dark eyes warm with lust,
undulating hips and bellies,
twining thighs and melting vulvas.
Who'd refuse them?

Squatting at their feet,
hot-eyed, ravenous ascetics,
naked, grey with dust and ashes,
worship greater

goddesses through pain:
beings of gigantic beauty,
calmly smiling, awesome in their
undulations.

Heavenly Bodies

As goddesses, cloud damsels, court ladies, demons, queens,
swarm in the nude on temple walls, their billowy breasts and thighs
involved in sacred mysteries
above the heads of awestruck devotees,
I picture the maharajah's wives playing between beds of lilies.

Naked in jewelled belts, warmed by the touch of his eyes
that shine like hidden suns through private screens,
they vie to display their pliant forms, the shapeliness and size
of breasts and quivering thighs, leaping as the flung ball flies,
pursuing one another, fleeing with shrill cries.

It's different in our gym.
When Miss Patel comes in,
strips to her vest and stretches, ready
– among suddenly self-conscious men –
to hone her abs, her glutes, her thighs,

though the mirror walls are alive with eyes,
her face is still as clear-cut stone; the lasers of her gaze
are locked on the figure straight ahead, the vision of herself,
pounding the treadmill belt to do her k's.

The World of Light

Though even before they've died
the tracks our loved ones leave in the brain
change, grow muddled and fade,
their traces will always remain.

When the last person to know
their faces in the drawer
of bleaching photographs
is himself no more,

when the human race has gone
and the planet turns to dust
or falls into the sun,
some residue will last,

while the visible forms of their bodies
will travel beams of light
between the stars forever
in interstellar night,

receding at a constant speed,
dwindling to infinity,
continuing in principle
when there's no one there to see.

Edmund Prestwich has retired from full-time
teaching to concentrate on writing. His latest book
is *Their Mountain Mother*, from Hearing Eye.

Derek Adams

Shrewd

I was somehow wrong:
(your point, well made and succinct)
you already knew this,
though I was yet to see
what any fool of a passer-by
who overheard the tiniest
snatch of conversation
could have told me
was obvious.

And the fact that I
was blinded by your
dazzling use of logic,
the way you took a thought
bounced it back and forth
like a Harlem Globetrotter
before spinning it on your finger
then placing it – Slam Dunk –
in the net.
'You can't argue with that!'

And I couldn't, couldn't
follow the ping pong words
that blurred before me,
concussed round my brain
as I tried to chase the echo,
retrace the labyrinthine path
back to your original statement, which
I was sure was somehow flawed
but it was like trying to follow footprints
on a beach volleyball court,
and I see now that
I am forced to admit
you are probably right
that the sun shines at night.

Seeing the Dead

Winking at me,
the cold light of stars
whose existence
was extinguished
millennia ago.

Through the six-inch mirror
of my telescope's
Newtonian reflector,
I see clearly
what is no longer there.

Tea leaves vortex through
luke warm liquid,
in a cup with a chipped lip,
the only warmth
in this long empty night.

Derek Adams is one of the organisers of the Essex Poetry Festival and also 'I Scream Sunday', a spoken word open-mic and alt art night in Chelmsford, Essex. Widely publish in the UK and abroad, he was a winner of BBC Wildlife Poet of the Year 2006. Collections include *unconcerned but not indifferent – the life of Man Ray* (2006), *Everyday Objects, Chance Remarks* (2005) and *Postcards to Olympus* (2004).

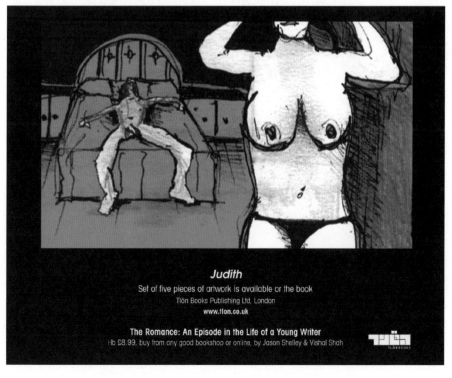

Vanessa Jackson

Woodcuts

Sam Riviere

Walter's Excerpt

Such as the instance recently, when Walter
found himself in want of company,
and later found himself at Frick's, a dive bar
on the freeway, its saloon doors headlit
by prides of trucks. There was a bar girl,
Beulah, with the limp of a straggler,
her excellent back criss-crossed with straps,
who Walter sweetly cajoled into cabbing home
and mixed gins for, and attacked, in the nicest way.

Having lost her earrings, raked his back to ribbons,
Beulah rose, her Bambi lashes dewy with sweat,
passed her drink-froze gaze over the room,
and decided on dislike. The reptiles were first,
bullied with stiletto spikes, then it was Walter's books
that drew her hexes. She stood before them scowling
as Walter groped for weapons. Then she simply
sighed *It ain't honest to multiply your life like that*

The Sisters of Allium

The onion lowered by my window
and shone into the room. Its white skin
tight with its own tang, these words
boomed from the closed bulb:

*You, Dupree, will use your useless cash
to hire much advertising space,
buy a caravan and start an all-girl band.*
I woke, milky tears dashed on my cheeks.

And no mistake, it was a sign –
I pestered talent scouts, plastered moons
in pissy underpasses. A jingle played on radio.
Sojourning in a lay-by, I watched the phone.

Soon the poor girls came, with pocked cheeks,
fruit-flavoured gum and sequinned jeans.
Each night one lay down with me,
the onion dowsing through my hand.

The town fathers heard of the auditions.
They drove out to talk to me
and found the costumes inappropriate:
white discs for bangles on the wrists

and ankles, slips thin as film
from onion skins. I was its willing servant,
but hardly accountable. Now, I'm back to scratch
with my harmonica, a choir of conmen,

and in this prison yard, the onion's quiet.
Underneath me, its children
are thinking softly in the soil.
Will you help me dig them out?

Honeymoon

Married – just – by the Caesar's Palace Bodhisattva,
my crown of flowers was flaking
and your pashmina grubbed the pavement
like torn toilet paper. 'This means we'll be rich,'
you said, 'and raise a set of sensitive sons.'

I cried when the clerk at Arabian Nights
jimmied open a locker of letters, sent my parents.
My parents were dead, or maybe abroad,
AWOL either way. I must have forgotten
I didn't know you that well.

I folded a cheque in my wallet
in place of a photo. The dude tamborined his keys
on his hip. 'We'll take the top floor,' I said.
'The highest,' you said, blowing smoke to your left.
I knew you approved.

'This means we'll outlive our peers,
die amused and alone in the Hollywood Hills.'
The elevator opened on Persia.
Carpets and mirrors were eating each other.
A vase sprouted white lilies,

'Symbolising marriage and death,' you said.
The ornament of an asp
biting through its own neck
was anyone's guess, but right then
an obscure source of comfort.

Sam Riviere was born in 1981. He co-edits
the anthology series *Stop Sharpening Your
Knives*, and is currently working towards
a PhD at the University of East Anglia. A
recipient of a 2009 Eric Gregory Award, his
Faber New Poets pamphlet is forthcoming
this summer.

Jim Burns

Drunks and Bankers

The middle of a warm afternoon,
and they're arm-in-arm, weaving
along the pavement. They're both
middle-aged and shabbily dressed.
the man carrying his jacket,
and showing an unpressed shirt,
the woman in stained jeans
and a top that once was clean.
They're smiling and singing,
exchanging a quick kiss,
oblivious to the rest of us
as we step out of their way.

'A bit of a state to be in,'
my companion says, and I reply,
'But they're happy, if only
for a day, or part of it,
so why deny them the right to be
that way?' My companion smiles,
and says, 'Trust you to defend them,
and if a couple of bankers
walked by, you'd sneer,' and I
answer, 'That's right, and the drunks
aren't bothering me today,
whereas tomorrow the bankers may.'

Consultation

They have a system known as
consultation, which means
that they make a decision,
then ask for our opinions
and tell us how welcome
they are, but we must abide
by the system, and the decision
is final, though they may,
in future, change the system,
subject, of course, to the
usual period of consultation.

A Close Family

The girl on the train
is telling her sister,
and her mother, what she'll do
to her boyfriend
if he goes with another woman.
'I'll cut his fucking balls off,'
she says, and the mother smiles,
and tells her own stories
of love and its infidelities.
They are clearly a close family,
and go on to share experiences
with vibrators, laughing loudly
and daring each other
to be more and more explicit.
The sister joins in,
a few extra four-letter words
colour the conversation,
while the rest of us
look anywhere but at them
and listen intently all the time.

All Experiences Are Useful

When my father and mother fell out,
which was often enough, they wouldn't
speak to each other, and instead
used me to communicate. They'd sit
on either side of the fire, and I'd
be on the carpet in between them,
playing with my toy soldiers,
and my mother would say, 'Ask your
father what he wants for his tea.'
I'd ask him, and he'd say, 'Tell your
mother I'll have bacon and egg.'
And so it would go on,
even for a few weeks at a time,
until some sort of truce was declared,
and I'd be spared any further need
to act as their go-between.
Did it have any effect on me?
Well, you could say that ever since
I've always valued silence
and using as few words as possible.

Her Response

'All I ever wanted to do,' he said,
'is make endless love to you.'

'Good God,' she said, 'You mean every day?
There's no way I could put up with that.

I mean, what about the kids and shopping,
and evenings out with our friends?'

'But think how wonderful it would be,'
he continued, 'Giving ourselves to it.'

'You must be joking,' she replied, 'and
what about washing the sheets from the bed,

what about earning a living, and what
about taking your hand off my leg?'

Farewell Message

'The writing is on the wall,'
he said, and by God, it was,
though not the writing we'd expected.

There were a lot of rude comments
about a woman we all knew,
and all the men she'd known.

And another which told us
what to do in no uncertain terms,
though it was anatomically impossible.

Then, finally, a brief comment
telling us why he was leaving.
The reason was beyond believing.

Jim Burns's most recent publication is *Streetsinger* (Shoestring Press).
He regularly reviews for Ambit.

Jehane Markham

Time is My Mind

Time is my mind
(and all the things that will happen or not)
The hyacinths sticking their curled heads out of the blue jug,
The cat pressed against the bottom door of the Rayburn.
Time is dust under the bed and unworn stockings curled in the drawers.
Time is smoke rising from the chimney and a new moon like a shrimp in the black
net of a tree.
Time is in the chickens scratching in the straw and the drip of water from the
outside tap.
Time is in the spindly, sprouting sweet peas.
Time is a baby asleep, face as blank as an uncooked cake.
Time is in the stiff tulips holding up their closed dishes of red and yellow before
breaking apart under the slow drag of opening days.
Time is trains and stations and being late, rushing like a storm of electrical
impulses towards something hard and slippery.
Time is the ticket collector waiting at the gate.
Time is the track, the lane and the road.
Time is the motorway from city to city.
It is the snake rising like a gloved finger from beneath the stone.
Time is my ego
(and all the things that will happen or not)
A crazy old tramp lifting up his head from the dustbin of my thoughts.
Time is a jug of dreams poured into me –
Don't stop.

Spring Equinox

On the dividing line
She died
When the first bees were climbing up the slopes of petals
She pulled in her fires
And put them out
One by one
All the lives in her disappeared
Like wild animals
We could not find her among the zoo-keepers and old folks
Only a stone effigy was left
In the clean, cream sheets
The warm she had slipped away
Between winter and spring
She had noticed the gap in the hedge and fled.

The Alphabet

How can I know you will stay till the end?
Not stifle a yawn, drift off,
Letting go my hand like a friend

Who suddenly remembers her own life,
The burdens and blocks in the bend
Waiting like bullies to scoff

At the inadequate hold of my mind.
There's so much I don't know,
The way the heart pumps the blood

The way the lungs inflate and blow.
Very basic things are hard to understand,
Even the alphabet stumbles at me,

A caravan of elephants crossing the sand.
Trunk by trunk, huge flapping ears,
Slow ballooning of leathery girth,

Each letter holding its own tears.
A train flashing over the land
As the seconds collect like flies on my nervous hand.

And the cows standing in green fields
Smooth as lead in creased positions
Of attendance and symbiosis to the weald.

Hedges are bustling with life and louse,
Braiding the hills with ancient vigour,
Catching birds in their sideways house.

Leaves are thrusting into light,
Filigrees of stalk and stem,
Thorns stick into flesh and white

Buds on the branch like pearls on a ruff,
The anthers dipped in pink,
Smell of wild honey, woodland stuff.

Once the alphabet was only just
A collection of feathers, bones, sticks,
Washed by the rain and dried to dust.

Before words there was only the shape of things:
An oval for an eye,
A boomerang for a mouth that sings.

Was it a Semite soldier who carved the first lines
Into sandstone two thousand BC,
Rising above Egyptian turquoise mines?

Now words make the world shared
In black patterns of relief,
War, pain, grief, love, beauty are all bared

In the small print under which we sink,
Travelling thousands of miles
As we cross our legs, blow our noses, blink.

Jehane Markham is a poet, lyricist and scriptwriter. She was commissioned to
write *On The Rim Of The World* by the ROH with composer Orlando Gough in 2009.
The Jehane Markham Trio performs poetry and jazz whenever it can.

Satyendra Srivastava

The Bhasmasur Love

Bone to bone,
Blood to blood,
Limb to limbs,
As if they were glued.
– Merseburg magic maxims

When love
Reaches its climax
– when it really does
It attains the ultimate
It could even perform
The final act
It could become a Bhasmasur
And burn itself to ashes
Like the demon himself
Who through great meditation
And sacrifice
Got the blessing of the god Shiva
And the power to burn anyone
By just putting his hand
On the person's head

Drunk with his power and love
He became infatuated
Almost obsessed
With the love of god Shiva's consort
And that was it
The other gods saw in this madness
In this love of a demon
For the goddess Pavarti
A peril
Which must be averted
They plotted against him and
Somehow tricked him into
Putting his hand on his own head
And that's what he did
And that's how
He burned himself alive.

So goes the story of Bhasmasur
It could be the story of love too

The War

This blood had a name
Relations
Godfathers territory
A mission and a priest
Followers with legitimised kids
With passports and fingerprints

When the clerk valued the worth
Of the deaths here
Examined the convicted
Read the script of the mock trials
His blood froze
Words vibrated and settled
Into the sweat on his forehead.

The crowd was getting paler too
Over the walls the baby snakes ran aimlessly
And then crept into the cornfields
Turning them blue

This is the land of the motivated
The blood their price
The draw of equals the winner's shield

Our globe of unequals will never understand
The echo of laughter flying all over
Telling the same story again and again
This is one war that never ends
This is one wall that never knows its boundary
And we the winners of medals
Honours and insignia still wonder
Why and for how long

Satyendra Srivastava was born in India. A well-established writer in Hindi, he has also published four collections of poetry in English: *Talking Sanskrit to Fallen Leaves* (Peepul Tree), *Between Thoughts* (Samvad), *Another Silence* (Samvad) and most recently *Sir Winston Churchill Knew My Mother* (Ambit Books). Since his retirement from Cambridge University where he lectured for twenty-five years he has travelled extensively, lecturing and reading his poetry.

Nina Bogin

The Old World

These towns, these places on the map,
come complete with auras, their names
resounding like chimes. Rivers and bridges,
steeples and the smell of ink. I look down
from the bell-towers and see, spiraled at my feet,
the vendors in the square, the cobbled streets
where the first editions were churned out,
rainwater flowing through the gutters to the sea.

Flocks of starlings fly up and up, winding me
into their legend, who once toiled in the fields
or, in the back alleys, scrubbed
blackened pots and pans,
never learned to read, and long ago
disappeared into a grave
where the Hebrew letters of my name
blend into the moss-covered stone of the land.

A Wheatfield

Our bodies are the color of wheat, in a field
alongside a river, where long-necked geese
spread out over the marshes, their wings carrying them
on spirals of wind. We too skimmed across
the world as we held each other, our skin sweet
with the scent of grass, warm from the sun that flooded
our mornings. And below us were the same green banks
tangled with violets and cowslips, the purple spikes of milkwort
that brought us, year in, year out, our awaited springs.
It can't be true that each day we are new, for each day
we are older, but we keep more and lose less,
and all the things we took no heed of – how fallen oak leaves
place themselves on beds of moss, how your body
marries the slope of mine – are as clear now as when
we first lay flank to flank and let ourselves be borne
to river-marshes, where wheat rippled in the sun,
where the geese tilted their long grey necks like rudders
and hoisted themselves into one blue V, honking
and calling as they spun out before us.

Nina Bogin was born in New York and has been a resident of France for over thirty years. She lives in north-eastern France, where she works as a translator and teaches English in an engineering school. Her two books of poetry are *In the North* (Graywolf) and *The Winter Orchards* (Anvil).

Romance with a Stick Insect SW7

Catherine Eisner

> And I, that never cared a straw for any manner of woman until now, I took to
> you when I thought ye were a boy.
> Robert Louis Stevenson – *The Black Arrow*

'One finger in the throat and one in the rectum makes a good diagnostician,'
my father mused, and looked up at me with an arched eyebrow.

I must have made a face.

He was kneeling, bowed over the rear of the robotic dog he and my cousin,
Vernon, had fabricated from relics long forgotten in the toy cupboard.

I had just turned fourteen and my mother had been dead a year. At that time we
lived on the garrison campus near my father's Department of Artificial Intelligence
and Applied Neural Computation.

'Now you're no longer a child, it's time to put away childish things,' Father
soothed, attempting to console me as he dismantled Happy, my mechanical
walking-talking dwarf, a present from Uncle Irving when I was four.

In naming their robotic dog their choice evoked the honoured memory of the
ill-fated Soviet space-dog who'd first orbited Earth, and from the throat of Laika Mk
II now issued the voice of Happy, reprogrammed for minimal smalltalk should the
automaton have cause to express synthetic emotion in human–robot interactions.

'I am Happy,' Laika announced in a racheted, shredded voice to all who
encountered it, and thus a new element now entered my life; a fresh rival rose
up to compete with me for my father's regard.

I was suddenly confronted by the basic dilemma of my adolescence: in a
household of men who could now understand or guide my inner life?

Certainly, my father the mathematician – newly appointed an Associate
Lecturer in Cognitive Robotics – was not interested in this strange freak of his.
Nor could I attempt to touch upon the question of my nascent under-formed
womanhood and painful conflict of emotions, which for my own part I found
as awkwardly indefinable as an irrational number, and as inexpressible as Pi.

My father claimed he regarded his adopted nephew as my 'spiritual foster-
brother', yet I am of the opinion that my cousin satisfied more nearly an elemental
longing for a primogenic son.

And, as he grew into his teens, Vernon began to resemble my father to an
astonishing degree! The toothpaste on the chin. Shaving foam on ear lobe.
Odd socks. Pockets bulged with metal solder and lengths of copper flex.

Both would use a shirt cuff as a jotter, never mind the table cloth.

There was a little spare room at the back of our garrison quarters and, in that
den, uncle and nephew would nibble Leibniz biscuits while they debated his
(Leibniz's) theorematic propositions with an intensity that gave my cousin no
opportunity for healthy inward growth through indulgent daydreams whose
aims should have been no more than delightfully futile.

Even when their mental sleeves were, as it were, rolled up for playful intellectual combat over the draughts board their minds continued to be tortured by a steely logic that excluded those elements of conventional knowledge necessary for everyday social usage.

But I did not envy Vernon. He examined all of life through the distorting lens of semantic mathematics, witness this early rudimentary sketch of his for a conceptual problem in propositional logic posed by his naive attempt to replicate the sensory input to the neural network of an Artificial Intelligence in improbable smooch mode.

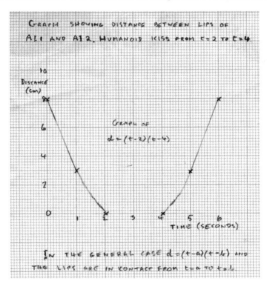

The enormous mass of closely printed figures and symbols needed to configure the logic circuitry for Laika Mk II never seemed to appal Vernon; the maze was always clear enough beneath such penetrating eyes.

From this you might rightly conclude that Vernon was marked down as my male twin: a *puer aeternus*, a perpetual teenager. True. My cousin was struck more by a robot's alien splendour than by a girl's full lips and supple arms.

'The human machine is not constructed to go always at high pressure,' my father observed during the early orientation trials of Laika Mk II. 'But our mechanical *Jägerhund*,' he boasted to Vernon, 'thrives on everything fate can throw at him.'

As to my own fate…had my father's rearing of us been different I might have thought more of myself and less of Vernon.

The revolution in my personal affairs took place on my eighth birthday, or more precisely when I reached the thirty-second year of my bloodless life. Because, you see, I am a leap year baby and, as a bissextile individual (*and* I'm compelled to remind you that 'bissextile' merely pertains to a leap year and not to feminine indeterminateness), I have further cause for feeling out of step with my compeers.

So the events in my early adulthood I am about to relate must appear altogether stranger for often being the outcome of deficiencies in my emotional responses so dimly apprehended at the time.

'*The only possible society is oneself*,' I consoled my bruised pride, which came of a knowledge that I was considered an animal of a different species, not accepted by the herd.

After a catastrophic annulled marriage, *matrimonium ratum non consummatum*, the hideous uncertainty had ended and my future was to spend my days with spinsters and the knitters in the sun.

Accordingly, as a salve to my wounded spirit, my father proposed I should join Uncle Irving, the celebrated bibliophile, at Albert Hall Mansions, and my hopes leapt at the thought of revisiting South Ken.

'In my borderland of *rus in urbe* we need be neither one thing nor the other, so long as we don't frighten the horses in Rotten Row,' Uncle Irving reasoned on the telephone.

So I accepted blindly.

But very soon Irving disabused me of any fanciful notions I'd entertained as to a simple life of seclusion expected by an anchoress; for it became clear I was to be offered the post of 'Girl Friday' in his bachelor's eyrie…a quasi-secretary-companion-cook-general-factotum and, what's more, his muse…a *muse* in a pageboy haircut and fringe.

My godfather was *very* particular about the clothes he wished me to wear in our new domestic arrangements together.

He took me to a Thameside ship-chandler where he bought me a pair of seaboots, ten pairs of woollen socks, a navy blue cotton guernsey, and five knitted cotton vests and jockey shorts. I was puzzled but unconcerned; since my early teens I've had no need for lingerie that's racily lacy.

On the journey home he confided certain secrets surrounding maleness that are shared by submariners. For example, I should pinch the edge of a razor blade to prolong its life. Oh. And, apparently, a *real man* opens his newspaper like a Hebraist, in the opposite direction, and reads the Sports pages from back to front.

In advancing age, my godfather was even more elusive in his hideaway, and all callers were discouraged with the strict abjurement that he'd gone to ground.

The fabled passion for his books remained, and his revived enthusiasm for photography found release in the portfolio of portraits he began to amass of his reluctant subject…his niece and helpmeet, the ardourless Stick Insect.

Irving confessed to a penchant for photographing me in all manner of coarse workwear, as if a solemn stablelad in riding boots or tame fisherboy with soulless grey-green eyes had wandered into the park.

He preferred his old Rolleiflex (bartered by a captured *Fregatten-Kapitän* for a carton of Chesterfields) because he liked the large square format of the film, and the image in the view-finder wasn't upside down.

'Everything's a bit realler when it isn't, for once, back to front,' he remarked during a long day of make-believe, as he framed his next shot. At the time, I was wearing a pair of WW2 German whipcord hunting breeches with rear buckle fastenings, which rather belied that assertion.

'Up in the clouds,' Irving would often declare. 'No better place for an alien soul to lift wings.'

Albert Hall Mansions SW7 are known as a Babylonian ziggurat of flats, and Irving's lofty duplex apartment had one of the finest views overlooking Hyde Park and Kensington Gardens.

His rooms were all gleaming mahogany and old red morocco, yet a third of the entire space was occupied by a solid mass of books. Volumes were stacked several rows deep against the walls and almost up to the ceiling. All the walls were papered in dark brown to better show off Irving's pictures.

When Vernon and I were thirteen, Irving surprised us both by proposing a 'cultural Grand Tour' of Europe; we'd disembark at Lisbon and he'd chart our course, unaided by compass, overland across the Midi to Venice, with only three Michelin stars to guide him.

On board our Cunard steamship out of Southampton, Vernon and I were objects of curiosity among admiring passengers due to our extraordinary similarity, which rendered gender indistinguishable. Irving had insisted we wear identical white shorts and Aertex sports shirts, and we were each given the same bob haircut.

'Deeds are male, words are female. Only men are lionised,' Irving assured me when I'd first protested at being taken for a boy. So I'd resolved to emulate Vernon in all things. I even, experimentally, taught myself to fearlessly strike a match *towards* my cigarette – just like a boy – instead of away from it.

'Nothing becomes him so well as cropped hair,' Irving remarked on the day we crossed the Italian border at Menton. He lighted his cigar at one of the spirit-lamps affixed to the restaurant's entrance pillars.

'*Persi, orfana anima*,' he observed.

From the dining terrace he was following keenly the progress of Vernon as my twin-cousin loped towards us, taking the steps three at a time.

'Lost orphan soul,' my godfather explained to me, but I felt it was I who was living those lost orphan hours, not Vernon.

As we approached the shop near the Ponte dei Tre Archi, I glanced up at the fascia:

Earl W. Smithews Jr
Philographer & General Antiquarian
Rare Books & Manuscripts • Libri rari e antichi veneziani

The bookseller greeted the two of us with the sign of a redskin brave.

'*How*, little lady,' he drawled teasingly. '*How*.'

Tall as my godfather was, Irving reached no higher than Earl's shoulder.

'C'mon, Slick! You owe me big for this,' Earl wheedled. He was a person whose tongue appeared too large for his mouth.

The bookseller led my godfather to a tall inlaid cabinet that stood between two windows, unlocked it, and withdrew a crown octavo volume with salmon-pink buckram boards. He gently removed a docket.

'Listen. Your head's gonna bust when you see this. It's beyond price. A lost

gem restored to the Wildean canon, and with your name in the codex.'

Below us, the waters of the Cannaregio canal sent ripples of light across the ceiling as a *vaporetto* passed under a bridge.

Earl adjusted his tortoise-shell spectacles and applied his silk handkerchief to the leaves of the book's top edge. On the cover was printed the title in a grumous red: *Lord Arthur Savile's Crime and Other Stories*.

Irving's eyes glittered with a reflex at the cold, white expanse of the uncut title page; for there's a distinct light that comes into the eyes of a passionate bibliophile at the mere mention of a flawless first edition.

'Ain't selling you short, I tell ya.' The bookseller withdrew a folded letter hidden snugly inside two uncut leaves.

'Any doubts, sir, as to its authorship, quite apart from the penscript, are gonna vanish once you've seen the content. You betcha!'

Sight of the letter drew from Irving a long, low sigh and I saw his lip quiver. He took the paper to the window and held it to the light to seek a watermark. Then he returned with warmth the book dealer's dry hard smile.

'Auld Oscar could be an Oirish dunce sometimes on the niceties of English punctuation.' Irving caught my eye. 'Had a habit of apostrophising possessive pronouns when everyone knows they're absent. Anyhow, Oscar's pen-stroke is about as restrained as a dyer's hand. Inimitable!'

Irving squeezed my shoulder with a strange fervour.

'When I'm dust, *this* shall be yours,' he said tantalisingly. 'In the end, all art shrivels to the trivial. But this *never*!'

He lovingly smoothed the page and refolded the letter. '*This* is by way of being more a holy relic.'

We followed Earl into his cramped office; he wore a faded Argyle cardigan draped over his shoulders and the sleeves hung from his back like the wings of a fallen angel.

'Impeccable provenance. Shall I wrap it to go?'

Irving leant against the stacked bookshelves and breathed rapidly. He scribbled a figure in dollars on his wrist.

'Aw, gee! Gimme a break!'

A wad of American Express travellers cheques changed hands.

'*Eccellente!*' My godfather stroked my close-cropped helmeted hair fondly. '*Bellissima.*'

Irving held with infinite care his prize as we crossed a bridge to a floating jetty.

'All art is emotional fraud!' he boomed. '*Provence and Troubadour are merest lies,*' he quoted.

He pointed to a woefully plain lady wearing fashionable butterfly sunglasses who was flitting from quay to quay under the amused gaze of the *gondolieri*. Her flared beach pyjamas, boiled incredibly white, glared in the sun.

'*Baby! Bébé! Bambinetto!*'

A little dog with the fluffiness of a day-old chick ran past.

My godfather stayed my impulse to follow with a pinch on my wrist.

'Wait here! The game's afoot!'

He drew me into the deep shade of an archway leading to a palazzo.
'Observe.'

The fluffy dog – a Lhasa Apso – leapt from the water's edge into the arms of a handsome young gondolier, in a felt hat with a twisted brim, who'd been enticing it with scraps spread on his *panino*.

Within a few seconds the dog's mistress joined them.

'Emotional fraud!' my godfather repeated. He spoke in a sort of basso buffo voice, comically taunting.

'Besides. See that barnet of hers?' He pointed to Peggy Guggenheim's unloosed streaming hair. 'It's dyed blacker than a witch's armpit.'

If a millionairess who'd reputedly bedded one thousand men, I thought, could snare a young lover with a small dog, then maybe the fascination these little creatures held for me was unwise.

I suffered dreadfully when Irving was reported missing, ten months after my arrival at Albert Hall Mansions. Our placid cohabitation had been all too fleeting.

The mansion block was searched for seven hours by the police.

One morning my godfather had set out to post some letters in Knightsbridge and had not returned.

For five years I was to remain faithfully in that curious set of apartments as housekeeper and curator; a hapless creature mired in her own fatuity and stricken by the sharpest self-torments.

Then, on my seventh birthday (in my twenty-eighth year!), when tinkering with Irving's study-keys, I opened a locked plan-chest, and found an album arranged with the photos my uncle had taken of me in the park; he'd dedicated the collection to his principal correspondent, Earl Smithews.

Oddly, a descriptive text had been drafted for each study, so apparently the album meant more to him than simply a scrapbook. Here is a typical entry, beneath a photo of me dozing in my mariner's guernsey at midday on a shallow bank of spring flowers (holding, no doubt, an exacting pose that had reduced me to torpor). I will not quote *in extenso*:

> *'Noontime Shore Leave'* – *Good Friday, April 9. Boy Friday*: Head half raised turned slant-wise, propped on one arm, ankles crossed, straight-toed feet; face unimpassioned, neat features; slender, thin-flanked, waistless; rounded skull, hair cropped close to nape, good teeth, column of throat tanned; flat pectorals; naive unusedness; see how an open deception exquisitely deceives!

Uncanny! That could have been my cousin Vernon outstretched in the photo!

In all my life I had never known what it was to truly invite admiration until that moment. No man since my lately decoupled *kibbutzniker* husband had so much as glanced in my direction.

According to Vernon, an 'imitation game' was proposed by the logician Alan Turing, the Father of Artificial Intelligence, in which a humanoid machine has to imitate a woman imitating a man yet convince observers it's of womankind, and leave no doubt as to which is the true human being.

At that instant, this intrusive thought recalled my father and the strange interrogation to which I was submitted on the night of my fourth birthday (I was sixteen).

My heart began to beat as it had never beaten before.

★

My birthday party had ended in inevitable disaster and I'd withdrawn to my room in a sulk, unwilling to endure the cackling yard hens who professed to be my school friends.

I was, therefore, extremely alarmed when, soon after my going to bed that night, my widower-papa came into my room with a pale face and searching eyes.

I was half sitting, half lying in bed, with the bedclothes sloping from my knees like some stodgy teenage hausfrau.

'I would wish you "Happy Birthday" but…'

'…in sixteen years I've never grown more than four years smarter!'

I did not switch on the lamp; only a little faint starlight entered by the window. I detected the odour of a serious talk in the atmosphere.

There was a blankness in his aspect. The light from the landing flashed off the lenses of his spectacles. They were like two blank white counters from his draughts board. What had I possibly done to earn his displeasure?

'I may as well tell you now. I want you to give him up. Your cousin, *Vernon*.'

I was suddenly numbed by a sickening sense of weakness.

'What you are saying?'

'I would not forgive myself if you and he…um…were to go generally to the bad.'

My cheeks reddened. My hands were hot, and my heart began thudding so powerfully that I could hear the ventricular '*lubb-dupp*' resounding in my bloodstream.

I was greatly wounded and offended. In all my troubled adolescence Vernon had held no ideas of an immoral nature. (For Christmas I would give him a gold tiepin, say, or initialled cuff-links; it was the only time in the year my cousin kissed my cheek.)

'That's so much hooey! You're dead wrong!' I protested at last in a low voice. 'We've known each other since we could first crawl, and we have always been good friends. That is all.'

There was a strange, hard ring in his tone as he echoed my words.

'Good friends? Of course,' he continued, 'I have seen it going on for a long time. I feared an attachment might form itself.'

'Absurd! I do not care for him in that way.'

My father seized my shoulder and I shrank back in pain.

'You are keeping something from me. Tell me! I insist on knowing.'

I burst out laughing.

'You're *so wrong*! Vernon expects nothing,' I groaned, 'because he knows I have nothing to give.'

My father, who had set out to mathematise the whole gamut of human feelings, had no conception I am certain of my pain at that moment. He was simply asking questions to which I had no reply.

'I know there's *something* between you,' he insisted.

82

He was looking fixedly at me, with his long tapering fingers nervously intertwined. Then, finger by finger, my father the inventor pulled off a pair of slate-coloured gloves (an exercise, incidentally, calculated to be the supreme challenge for mimetic dexterity in humanoid robotics).

I felt at a loss, abashed, unequal to the moment; he'd charged his last remark with a weight of significance.

'You mean you suspect I might seduce him…even while I'm on the shelf?'

'Essentially so.'

I laughed again. I did not have the depths to be tragic.

'It never entered my head.'

'Can't you see I have only your interests at heart? There is the whole question and the whole answer. *Vernon is officially off-limits.*'

He was holding up his cheek in an absent way for his goodnight kiss.

I kissed him. At a stroke all the light had gone out of my life.

My father was regarding me oddly.

'What?' I smiled somewhat tearfully.

'The way you smiled then seemed to remind me of…'

'Who?'

My father, Associate Lecturer in Cognitive Robotics and Artificial Intelligence, stroked his chin, genuinely perplexed.

He shook his head as if to restore a loose connection, then, still puzzled, turned away, a shadow of a thought in his eyes.

'I can't imagine what I was thinking.'

It was as though Geppetto the woodcarver had chastised his marionette, Pinocchio, for sexual misconduct and expected to draw blood.

Since my mother's death, any memory of our family's distinct history and characteristics had been, I felt, sucked from our identities and swallowed by some supermassive black hole in a distant galaxy.

Once, I asked my father to recall my mother's real presence and essence.

'Her face is as familiar to me now as my army service number,' said the abstracted mathematician, lowering his pen over proof-sheets on his desk.

So, after the disturbing episode in my bedroom, I no longer asked myself why my father had insisted, with a fixation peculiar to himself, on the singularity of prime numbers for the location of our army quarters in Ordnance Alley on the Stoneburgh campus.

No. 35, as Vernon spelled out in terms opaquely obscure to me, was composed of consecutive primes, known as 'twin primes'.

Nor did I continue to puzzle over the fingerpost that pointed to our side of the alley, which read, *Odds*.

I might have remained tormented by my ignorance of my ancestry had not the answer by the queerest chance presented itself.

Terrible to relate (or *horribile dictu* as Irving would say), four more years were to pass before the fate of Irving's estate was known by his executors, when his halfskeletonised corpse was found in his wine cellar, hidden by one of his travelling-trunks; workmen, at the time, had been repairing the humidors.

A bottle of Schnapps and several farewell letters lay next to the remains. His identity was established through dental records, though his toupee had survived him practically intact.

In his long absence, I'd returned to pennilessness without a protector. To earn a bare subsistence I used to drudge away, walking our neighbours' dogs; but only those fashionable little creatures that had been neutered. Spayed bitches are so much more submissive without their oestrus cycle.

Quite honestly, when I observed their docile behaviour, I often felt I was little more than an animal myself, with the gift of speech.

I read recently that researchers in Dubois, Idaho, have discovered a strain of asexual sheep: creatures of negligible sexual heat.

Mostly I feel no different from Duboisian sheep.

In the end I owed my fortune to the beneficence of my godfather for I was declared his sole heiress.

Irving's apartment, its contents and *rariora* were mine.

Clearly my godfather had truly loved me, had actually adored my uneasy femininity, had admired my boy-like symmetry, my even teeth, my pastoral undevelopedness, indeed, had liked most of my qualities excepting the single fact that I was not a boy, but a girl.

And as he wrote, in that last letter to me:

Bon sang ne saurait mentir! You're the very image of your father. A subtle divergence of character, perhaps, but such a strong personal resemblance! The same look as your father's twin sister, Euphemia. It was a terrible thing! To die unreconciled to her twin brother! Divorce was a shameful admission when we were children. Father took off with your papa and me. Your grand-mother stole away with little Effie overseas – siblings separated when barely toothed. Half our family became dead to us. Mother punished Father with a lifetime of keeping the twins apart.

Unreconciled? Twin sister?

I wanted to recall Irving from the grave and shout: '*Do you mean to tell me that in all that time the twins never met!?*'

Astonishingly, I could only conclude that my father had harboured impure thoughts for his estranged twin sister as she grew to maturity in some kind a paral-lel universe of his mind, the product of the wildest poly-cosmic theorising of which he was only vaguely aware.

How else to account for the perverse suspicions that had crept into his thoughts to slander Vernon and myself? Or else explain the absurdity of my father behaving like some holy rolling preacher warning of Satan's traps?

Perhaps there was in the rhythm of my movements some subtle resemblance to the movements of his imagined sister?

I could see luminously now and understood the confusion of immature impressions and contradictory desires that had fashioned the child I once was, incapable of the smallest independent action.

All the same, *I knew*! Few things are more disappointing than complete success.

I regret immeasurably, with an unassuageable guilt, that in Irving's last days I had never associated his mysterious weight loss and waxen skin with the advance of his kidney disease.

Of all my inheritance the most cherished bequest was that crown octavo volume in salmon-pink I'd observed my uncle purchase in Venice when I was thirteen. That Irving, the renowned bibliophile, had *not* dismissed that letter in Oscar Wilde's own hand as a fake is revealed in the little note addressed to me, which accompanied the gift. The tone is entirely characteristic:

> As darling Oscarino tells us, 'To censure an artist for a forgery is to confuse
> an ethical problem with an aesthetical one.' Ha bloody ha!

Irving subscribed to a discreet mode of campery that sometimes found voice. As Earl Smithews remarked of Irving, quoted in the *Times* obituary: '*The world of bibliophily is full of crazies yet Irving's was the voice of the lovely sane.*'

Readers must judge for themselves the basis for my godfather's belief in the authenticity of the holograph document, appended below. Charles Matthews, the dedicatee, was Oscar Wilde's legal counsel on the day of the arrest of the Irish playwright in Room 118, at the Cadogan Hotel, after being accused of gross indecency following his libel case against the Marquess of Queensberry. The date was Friday, April 5th, 1895; and one might speculate that the verse was composed in the early dawn of the following day in the prisoner's cell at Bow Street police station.

It is as though, over the dead centuries, the hollow exculpatory verse is addressed to me alone.

David's Lyre Music
for Jonathan

The greatest beauty is unenjoyed.
On fruit ungarnered from the stem
falls dew from dawns as unalloyed
as lips unkissed whose savage charm
is stainlessly uncharactered
by the corruptibility of self regard.

The future is a book with seven locks, and I have opened six of them.

The *année bissextile* of my thirty-second year fell on a Friday. Thirty-two years is the traditional age of the *Christus Mortuus* and the day arrives as a reproach, I think, to remind us to question the failure of our own ministry on earth.

I would sit opposite my godfather's empty chair on the smaller footstool with clasped, guilty hands; I blame myself for failing him; but who's to say when Irving crossed the barrier which divides the sane from the insane?

(Sometimes, if I was seated on my footstool, he would toss a matchbox at my lap, and nod with approval when I caught it, as he had taught me, gripped between my knees.)

It's true the instances of his eccentricities were many.

When I first arrived at the apartment, Uncle Irving took me over the two suites of rooms. As we came down a flight of stairs, he suddenly pointed to a wall, and said:

'You'd say,' I'd expect, little girly, that this is the end of our domain?'

'I would.'

'Let us see.' He pressed a concealed button. A false door slid back and there was his vast fireproof library, with a high fretted ceiling, leading to a rumpus room where his rubber frogmen's suits were stored.

His secret jib door resembled a shallow glazed library cabinet with ebony inlays and brass grilles. A double falsehood was effected by the trompe l'oeil contents of the shelves: lost, destroyed or unwritten books with impossible titles on their spines…*Memoirs* by Lord Byron, *Journals 1865–1890* by Sir Richard Francis Burton and *Love's Labour's Won* by William Shakespeare.

The recesses, sliding panels and secret passages in those apartments would have baffled the skill of the most hardened safecracker.

These levels of subterfuge extended to his private conduct, I thought, when I remembered his life of constant duplicity; how could he have helped me when his only dictum was to drink life to the lees?

★

On that Friday of my eighth bissextile year, I sat at my balcony looking out upon Hyde Park. Beside me, in the shade of the parapet, grew a barren quince tree, root-bound in a tub.

In the reception room, mirrored by the glass French doors, I could see Vernon and my father working with the alacrity of ants on their robotic dog, Laika Mk IX.

They had just returned from a robotics seminar at the Imperial College in Exhibition Road.

My father was looking paler and darker eyed than usual.

There was a hush around them, a dead silence for a while – the paralysing kind of hush that broods on the worst that can befall you before it happens.

I could hear only their breathing.

Then, my father turned and searched my face with a forbidding air as if I were a fairground booth exhibit.

I must have worn the blank look of curious density that children adopt in order to avoid receiving hateful adult impressions; my face was a dead wall.

Vernon pressed a button and immediately the mechanical dog's jaw fell to its usual degree of set depression and apathy. It then hiccoughed.

Vernon had tried to explain their Laika Project to me once.

'We believe the actions of the human brain are reducible to the mechanical process so, according the Uncertainty Principle, even error should be admitted as a function of Artificial Intelligence. That's the paradox of cybernetical machines. A flaw in a program can point the way to its perfection.'

The mechanical dog continued hiccoughing.

'Every dog has its day, but that day has not come,' I heard my father, the bloodless logician, concede with a face of pained disappointment.

Their goal, all those years, had been to create a sentient automaton that can perform tasks exceeding those defined by Category Five of Human – Robot Interaction in demonstration of higher-level Artificial Intelligence techniques.

'Decisional autonomy', is also the aim, Vernon once told me, with Laika IX programmed to acquire the knack of 'Perceptual Learning, Spatial Reasoning, Object Recognition, and Disambiguating Human Relationships,' as well as configured to 'derive human intent from speech, gestures, body language and facial expressions.'

I opened the balcony door a little wider and called lightly to Vernon.

'Pee-arrum-ublum?'

As I've attempted to explain, there was a special attachment – as powerful as identical twins – between Vernon and myself as children…so intimate we would finish each other's sentences. We invented our own private language which we called 'Ennumohwuns'. We loved writing mysterious letters in this made-up language and exchanged them in secret.

Vernon gazed in his silent, emotionless way, with no look of animation in his eyes. We share the same black line round our grey-green irides.

There was an almost imperceptible shrug of his shoulders then my cousin glanced towards me beneath his dark lashes, and answered.

'Deeum-oggums ess-ummays, "En-yetum pee-arrum-ublum!"' He grinned.

The robotic dog shook its head confounded. I noticed a metal hinged panel near its rump was stamped, *BRITISH THROUGHOUT*.

The dog delivered another hiccough with a faultless intonation in which no ring of human emotion could have been detected, even by ears much finer than mine attuned to the nuances of social converse.

It had been three months since I'd last spoken to Vernon, to thank him for his artfully fashioned Christmas card, a bright green Truth Logic circuit-board for computer processing with Yes-Gates and No-Gates in the shape of a reindeer, terminating in a red light-emitting diode.

A church bell in Knightsbridge chimed five o'clock.

My tea party commenced at six and I saw the charwoman was setting the table and sideboard in the dining room; she had agreed to prepare a cold collation providing there were no dishes with foreign names.

My father opened his fob-watch and snapped his finger and thumb.

Vernon nodded and produced two neckties from his pocket.

'Now, now, Pappi. Remember, we agreed. Tonight we both have to choke.'

My mother had encouraged the infant Vernon to address my papa thus (and for years she had mistakenly called the little boy 'Werner'). Yet, until Mutti's death, I'd enjoyed a moderately happy child-life with no painful history; even while my mother had yearned for the thermal springs of Bad Oeynhausen, her baptismal home town (for there is no greater pain than to remember happiness in the midst of misery).

Soon my father was reluctantly drawing his necktie through his fingers with jerky, unnatural movements. He turned with a peculiar motion of the throat, as if swallowing something unpleasant, and studied me gravely.

'No need to be flurried, dearest, we'll be with you very soon.'

My face must have been flushed. My hot, illogical mood had brought about a revival of my old resentment against the strange kinship of that wifeless man, my father, and Vernon, the motherless boy…an orphan of the storm.

My father's attempt to soothe was in the manner of one making a prepared speech for a foreseen emergency; whereas, it was not in Vernon's nature to utter the customary trite consolatory or hopelessly hopeful remark.

Now my father sped with long strides towards me across the room.

He could not see beyond the quince tree and was unaware I was wearing a pair of tight-fitting shooting breeks that had been for Uncle Irving a particular favourite.

My father laid his hand upon my wrist. There was a subtle strangeness in his manner. His look was as different as possible from the fatherly glance he had once bestowed on me.

'Have you nothing to tell me, dear?' he inquired. 'Nothing to say?'

'No, but YOU have,' I seethed silently, without looking up, 'you have something to say on which you'll choke.'

For this evening I was the self I'd learned to be – hard, scornful, recriminatory.

Then my features twisted into a stereotyped smile of well-bred interest, as I observed a due sense of social formula.

I faced the two blank highlights of his specs.

'Please,' I said hastily, withdrawing my hand from his, 'we need not speak a word till we've all finished tea.'

With a nervous shift of pace, as of a person who summons the will to recover a wavering balance, my father laughed in his peculiar short way.

I knew his impassive face so well that I could read where most would have seen an unwritten page. He was observing every sign of my reaction.

Even at this moment his habit of studying and dissecting the functioning of the human mind was not laid aside.

'Of course,' he said. 'The next move is entirely yours.'

'Yes,' I granted on reflection, '*naturally it follows that my family should receive half my inheritance. Without question. But I hadn't expected them to ASK!*'

Anyhow, such was Vernon's extraordinary genius, the army had created a special civilian sinecure for him with security of tenure and pension rights.

For Vernon has prospered in his studies, so far as I can prove it to be so.

Since his early schooldays of brilliant promise, his career has risen like a rocket, while I…well…*I* have fallen like the *stick*, the stick the Stick Insect was so designedly bred to be.

Having slipped out of the apartment, I sat on a mossy mound at the foot of a huge maple tree in the park. I was in the habit of sitting there on the soft turf;

a private place to think. This steep turfed hillock in sight of my balcony smelled of evening dampness.

I was reluctant to proclaim myself the sole and single frump at my own party, so I sat there – an outcast, an Ishmaelite – as I pondered my ridiculous, stagnant existence.

I was wearing a paper party hat and a fine diamond choker, with a lattice-work of seed pearls, once worn by my mother; my only keepsake.

Curiously, I was beginning to comprehend how I might resemble the Stick Insect in one other respect, with an attribute to rival my wooden heart.

Protective colouring.

In the company of men, a degree of cunning over the years had conveyed I was a woman totally incapable of managing my own affairs, and powerless to act for myself.

'She's gotta good head on her,' I remember my husband once boasted in Biedak's restaurant, as though I were a child. 'A regella expert for figure-work, *mayn libling*,' he'd added with uncustomary tenderness.

There is no apparent reason why some words should be so distinctly remembered while others pass away from recall, yet I cannot forget that moment as I sat there, looking back at the lights of Irving's apartment.

Someone had found Uncle Irving's radiogram and his Cole Porter records; and Vernon was performing a comic moon dance with all frenzy of a solitary cosmonaut.

I want to ride to the ridge where the west commences,
And gaze at the moon till I lose my senses… Poppa, don't fence me in.

My bringing-up, my motherlessness, all the schooling I'd received had served only to remind me that I'd always have the greatest difficulty in persuading myself I could ever be happy, for I recognised I'd never formed any definite idea of what I could be. It was as if I'd been concealed in a garment so patched up that the original pattern had disappeared.

Anyhow, whatever the case, there is no cure for inamourable, unthawable frigidity, for a Duboisian asexuality, for the *execrabilis familia pathicorum* Irving spoke of so often.

I am sick at heart when I recall those words today. A pathic family indeed!

Mostly I wished someone would take all my blood volume and replace through transfusions whatever was bad within me.

Let me be by myself in the evenin' breeze… don't fence me in.

The music re-echoed from the Albert Hall piazza.

Silhouetted against the light streaming from the French doors, my father now circled Vernon in a strange shadow dance on the balcony.

All my life, I thought savagely, the Stick Insect had danced to their tune in their bizarre experiments to map the spatio-temporal matrix of human interactions, but now it was their turn to take *their* time from *me*.

I listened intently. A distant crackle of dry leaves beneath a hesitant tread repeated itself. Whoever approached did not know the way.

The moon hung like a riven dish.

I had an image of myself kneeling, head bowed, immersed in a pool of silver, my hair washed by cold moonlight.

Presently the colours deepened, and the evening came on.

The church bells rang; Friday evening was bell ringing practice night.

Ding-dang-dong!

And-so-on (or *Und so weiter*, as Mutti would say).

A twig snapped.

I swung round so fast my pearls spilled into my lap.

The dog, Laika IX, having successfully negotiated the path through the park to reach the maple tree, had apparently been programmed to bring me a plate of chocolate Leibniz biscuits.

The dull eyes had lost all light of intelligence.

It extended a hard, metal paw.

I kicked the machine with a pang of self-reproach as if I had struck some defenceless dumb animal.

I played with a Leibniz biscuit while I heard again the racheted, shredded voice scraped from the mechanical voice box, and the wheezing from the ironclad thorax, like the clearing of a rusted throat, as the program returned to its default mode.

'I am happy,' it rasped in its strangely metallic voice with more animation than I could ever summon. 'Are you happy, too?'

Catherine Eisner writes: 'The unique psychogeography (to employ a fashionable term) of Albertopolis SW7, which I attempt to probe in my text, is explored to remind us of the particular debt of gratitude owed by Royal College of Art alumni to this special place. It is also the spiritual home of many of *Ambit*'s celebrated contributors: Eduardo Paolozzi, Allen Jones, Peter Blake, David Hockney, Mike Foreman, Chris Orr...the honour roll is possibly too long to list for equity of inclusion...however, the alumnae of Astrid Chesney and Orly Orbach I mention with admiration.'

AMBIT No. 1
Andie Ferguson was Ambit's first art editor. He turned up at our first meeting, already having knocked up a fantastic sketch for the cover, which was pretty much perfect. Three months later Martin went to collect it, only to find that he'd thrown it out what he'd brought to show us as a rough draft. He re-drew what we could remember. Later he produced the blocked masthead that we are using again on the cover of this issue. Full of ideas, he went back to Australia and we lost touch, but he was Ambit's first visual ideas man.

Gerald Locklin

Pierre Auguste Renoir: *Dance at Bougeral*

My God, the rake who posed for this
Is dead set on seducing
The conflicted model
(Former trapeze artist)
Whose torso he draws into his,
Whose pink lips breathe mere inches from
His red-bearded, ruddy countenance.

He wants her and you know
That he will have her,
As he's confidently bedded
Scores before her.

Now, at a closer look, I see
That he's already pressing his groin
Into hers.

Look at her hand on the back
Of his neck;
Look at her right hand
Helpless in his grasp.

Eros is frightening in its intensity
To those possessed by it – the chosen few –
And those who wish they were – those many
Who may never be.

Boucher: *Venus Disarming Cupid, 1851*

This Cupid is one ugly runt.
There's no way that his pygmy wings
Could elevate his early-onset chub-besity.
My wife suggests his bloody buttocks
Might be caused by diaper rash.
The face of an angel?
More that of a pugilist.
In general, his epidermis has been
Tinted with and tainted by
The most hideous red on the palette.

In contrast (deliberately?) this is perhaps
The most lovely of the Venuses.
If indeed it is Madame de Pompadour,
Only recently furloughed as consort of Louis XV,
Then it is indeed a good thing to be king,
And the artist does indeed enhance her re-invention
As a Vestal Virgin. Her tiny nipples, on barely discernible
Areolae, are the pale pink of her lips and even paler cheeks.
(I bet her labia are too.) Her limbs are of flesh, but
Minimally muscled: No royal health-club regimen

For her century of courtesans. A slender thumb and
Forefinger have turned the point of the dart
Back at Cupid. The gentlest breeze softens her curls.
She is bemused by carnal love and has survived it,
Unscathed, unscarred, indelibly untouched…
And in no need of tattoos. J.-Patrice Marandel
Credits 'her success with the king' to 'Fidelity and
Discretion'. I'd guess a little of both would go a long
Way in our own time. A white dove at her foot
Reclines subserviently beneath the beak of her mate.
And yet who truly ruled the roost?

The benevolence of her smile,
The empyrean blue of the white goddess,
The embrace of her powerful thighs,
A string of precious pearls as pledge of exclusivity –
Who would not abandon all to be disarmed by
Her submission, vanquished by the conquest of
The most intimate beauty ever consecrated.

Roy Lichtenstein: *Girl with Ball, 1961*

Naturally the catalog claims
The artifice of the technique 'robs
Her of any sex appeal
She ever had.'

What does the art world
Know about sex appeal?
If she appeals sexually to me,
Then by definition she is not
Devoid of sex appeal.

And why else is she on the cover
Of the MOMA Highlights guidebook?
And on posters for miles around?

As she lifts the beach ball
Above her head, her breast rises also,
And I know her nipples feel
The friction of her bathing suit.
Her waist grows ever narrower,
And her hair waves in the wind.
So what if her round red mouth
Is 'doll-like'? Barbie is not only
'Doll-like', she's an actual fucking doll.
And the only men who mind that
Are the self-appointed social critics.

While they carp, I will be
Tickling her salty underarms
With my tongue, and nibbling on
Her tender, vulnerable neck.

Hope

The breasts of the Hope Hygeia –
In fact her entire body –
Are swathed in layers of cloth,
And, just for good measure,
She's wrapped her virtue in a serpent.
Not much hope there.

The garments of the Hope Athena
Would keep an Inuit warm in December,
Would deflect a rocket-launch assault,
Would foil Zeus on a Swan's Night Out –
And I'm not in His class.

But Bertie Thorvaldsen's Hebe,
A mere handmaiden, offers me her naked breasts,
Her uncommonly petite femininity,
Transparent skirt, bare feet, downcast gaze,
A cup and carafe of the purest spring water.
And, just for me, her putative virginity.

Gerald Locklin is Professor Emeritus at California State University, Long Beach, and
a part-time lecturer at both CSULB and the University of Southern California. His
most recent books include *The Dodger's Retirement Party: A Novella* (Aortic Press);
New and Selected Poems and *New and Selected Stories* (both World Parade Books).
Gerald Locklin: a Critical Introduction, edited by Michael Basinski (BlazeVOX Press)
is a collection of essays about his work.

Ron Sandford

A Sacred Grove – Cousins of Daphne

Sonja Besford

Arnica Talking

in the rucksack of a beautiful actress i knew
(as indeed she knew me and healed with me
many bruises, swellings and wounds)
long, long ago i sailed on the river niger
from ansongo through deserts and savannas
down jebba and further on to the niger's delta;
fires sparkled lighting swaying bushes
stars trembled above the thorny acacia trees
while velvety bats swooped to feed
on the sleeping fulanis' skeletal cattle, but nothing
nothing in that restless and throbbing beauty
disturbed the hausas' prayers or my actress's
allegiance to the bruised ego of her (real) prince
(white and exiled as only white princes were)
whose family raged against his foolish liaisons
with fickle ballerinas and amusing thespians
rather than marry any blue-blood, noble bitch;

let's find a treasure, the prince said to my actress.
so soon we were melting under the african sun
then solidifying under the desert moon –
in that land of everything old, the prince and his friends
laughed when killing, even more after killing,
hoping to stagger upon hidden gold masks and diamonds
while steeping their regal livers in brandy and wine –
even if i could have uttered human words,
the gentle actress would not have heard my warnings
for she loved her prince as tyrants love terror,
as prophets love prophecies, witch doctors chicken bones,
opium and heroin smokers oblivion –
i suppose, in his lust, he loved her as well, especially
in front of his coat of arms as if to mock its roaring lion
until we arrived in benin city where he dumped her –
there we became a semi-colon in the journal of his life,
my loving actress, her future child and i;
even if i could have cried resistance, there was no one
to hear it, we were all alone in her despair and although
i am mighty, the very first among healers, those humans
who contend my good forces also know that i am toxic
as indeed i was to my beautiful actress and her no future child

Meeting at a Party

immediately upon entering i saw him facing a mirror,
glancing regularly at his image, his eyes reflecting
self-adoring astonishment at his own perfection
as if the bleached teeth and manicured nails – so polished
that their glow danced in tune with champagne bubbles –
took him by surprise and held him forever perplexed:
i shook and swayed with my legendary cayenne anger
buried within the epidermis and with difficulty held
from bursting out by the prickle-cell layer
and its complicated bridges and spines,
for i remembered him when he was a revered prophet
with an enduring legacy of many true divinations,
a humble servant to gods and deities all the guests
present that night had worshipped eleven lives ago,
the journey we had all travelled but few could recall fully –
i wanted to hit and distort that faultless profile,
to break those competent hands, smash those elegant
fingers, ride a calash through his brain and startle it
awake by screaming or singing high, i wanted
to shake him back into a memory of his wisdom,
into his mysticism and into the enigmatic me
whom he loved move than the eleventh life itself
and thus he suddenly chose to leave it and me
for he was allowed only to love us all equally,
was forbidden to cherish one above all others:
guilty, he could not keep our horrible and lovely secret;
so i remained, delirious in my sadness, desperate
for the pleasures his body and mind gave me,
oh, i endured well by dreaming about him, seeing him
in every lover, teaching each one to caress me as he did,
to move with me as we used to;
i was willing and praying for the completion of that life
which came soon probably as a reward for all my lives
having loved in ways lacking in the modesty or timidity
given only to chosen women, but that night,
in the midst of my living the lonely new life
still remembering him, still loving him, still dreaming
his words, his sermons and his love making,
that night i was a furious witness to the gods playing
mischievously with our destinies
(perhaps even humorously, i thought)
as i watched that vain fool starting his new cycle
all over again with all the pomp and unblushing arrogance
of loving himself entirely and only

Sonia Besford was born in
Belgrade and lives in London.
These poems are from her
forthcoming eighth book,
Listener[3]. She is also working
with a translator, Jasna
Djurovic, on a book of Selected
Poems to be published in
Serbian later this year.

Julian Stannard

Diachronic Time

This is not diachronic time, this is pram in the garden time.
There's a rather large weeping ash out there
and it's being blown around by an August wind.
There's a pram under the tree with a white net over it
which will keep that old-fashioned baby far from harm.
The wind is blowing hard but it's a warm wind
and the baby which is sleeping, ah, what a wonderful baby!
is beginning to cry, and it's moving those little arms
and those little legs up and down and up and down.
When I next look in the pram it is completely empty
but now there's a baby in it, and now it is empty.
Baby, empty, baby, dog – I think it's a Jack Russell.

I believe we're watching cricket at the Oval.
Mr Boycott's coming in with a banana swinger
and look there's Peter May! Or is it Colin Cowdray?
I'm sitting next to my mother and she's holding
a rather large box of smoked salmon
because tomorrow my sister's going to be married.

Portrait of Isabel Rawsthorne Standing in a Street in Soho

Birth, and copulation, and death.
That's all the facts when you come to the brass tacks.
Birth, and copulation, and death

and a black forest blanched with frost
and a sheep maybe, and a walk along the street
and going to the butcher's for a chop

and coming back with *osso buco*
and a little tip-tap on the corner
if it doesn't look easy you aren't working hard enough.

And bumping into Isabel Rawsthorne
who's standing in a street in Soho
who doesn't look very well somehow

who looks as if she's lost her keys
who looks as if she's lost her foot
who looks as if her face's gone awol.
Hi Isabel, I say, I've got a bag of *osso buco*.
I wanted to buy a chop or a little bacon
but I ended up with *osso buco*.

Vonnegut's Dresden

The first fancy city I'd ever seen –
a city full of zoos and statues.
We were living in a slaughterhouse,
a nice new cement-block hog barn.

Mornings we worked in a malt syrup factory.
The syrup was for pregnant women.
The damned sirens would go off
and we'd hear some city getting it bad
whump whump whump whump.

We thought we were safe.
There weren't any shelters in our town,
just clarinet factories.
Then the sirens went; February 13th, 1945.

We went down two stories
below the pavement into a big meat locker.
It was cool there,
all those cadavers hanging around.
When we came up the city was gone.

Julian Stannard's next collection, *The Parrots of Villa Gruber Discover Lapis Lazuli*,
will be published by Salmon Poetry in 2011.

The Billboard Men

Jonathan Lethem

Night and the subliminal city

By night (though it was as bright at midnight as at noon) Salem and Marlboro had begun converting the billboards to better reflect the recent mood of the time-ruined city. They forged a language to describe the city's fugitive pockets of mercenary industry, those portable stalls of black market wares that flared up and vanished at the side of the highway without warning, stalls selling items both necessary and absurd: glass doorknobs mounted on walking sticks, useless princess telephones, bundles of multi-hued television cable and flamboyant pre-knotted neckties, t-shirts bearing the images of forgotten cartoon stars, grapefruits and oranges permanently on fire. Though the city was painstakingly dying – and indeed Salem and Marlboro found they could travel vast miles of elevated asphalt with no visible indication of the life that still scurried on the widening avenues below – it had far from emptied entirely. The city was in fact expanding across the desert, in the manner of the galaxy itself, the bleached-bone spaces that had always underlain the vast human out-cropping now rising up between the stretches of paving, between the flat-topped, sun-worn buildings, between the fields of parked or abandoned cars. Tides of com-merce had long ago thrown up the improbable oasis of steel and concrete on this parched desert, had rerouted rivers and commanded the water to sustain the lives here for a time, and then time and the waters had come to a halt, the sun frozen at perihelion in the sky. Now, in this long dying, it might be the commercial impulse that would outlive the city itself.

Salem and Marlboro worked in silent tandem, the instinct and understanding quick between them, and with no fear of exposure for the period it took them to com-plete the alterations. Like plastic surgeons the two carved differences into the grin-ning faces that beckoned to the absented highways. They found it surprisingly easy to uncover the cravenness just below the surface, the subcutaneous accusations and complicity inside the seductions, as though the billboards' own self-reproach had had actually ached be freed. Elsewhere they merely echoed the non-sequiturs of life in the amnesiac suburbs, making surrealist enunciation out of what no one even remembered well enough to take for granted: the maps and place names of the defunct empire, the charts and graphs of the business elites, the textbook illustra-tions and dissection diagrams of the absconded natural sciences. Material was any-where they looked. Everything they tried worked.

Returning to the billboards days and weeks after an intervention, Salem and Marl-boro frequently found testament to the persuasive power still residing in the medium, and to their ability to capture and redirect it: little honorific shrines of cac-tus and cabbages, arranged as if gazing upward at the advertisements, or small encampments of stubbed cigarettes and crushed beer cans, where bands of rovers had stopped to contemplate or briefly worship at their results.

A beseeching comes across the sky

Kent was lodged as usual in a tremendous traffic jam, speck in a flotilla of cars that crept like some great windless island of kelp and plastic flotsam caught in the ocean's stream, the first time he noticed one of the billboards, the ones that seemed to have him particularly in mind. You're Living All Over Me. We Make You Us. Every Good Reason Is No Longer Enough. My Best Friend Is Trying To Kill Me. More and more lately Kent seemed to live in his car, his apartment an adjunct, a kind of garage for his driver's body, his true life and the true life of the city actually taking place on the overpasses, the ostensible byways from one ebbing destination or another. The value of arrival diminished daily. What mattered were the products one could adapt to use inside the vehicle itself, and also those items one could acquire without exiting the freeway system, at the monstrous commercial pull-offs, which had become like identical Potempkin Villages themselves, false fronts where life could be enacted if one didn't examine the details too closely. Drive-thru windows were most perfect of all, and someday, Kent envisioned, he'd be able to make purchases without even slowing to a stop. Or was it one of the uncanny billboards that had made that prediction? Whose News Abuses You? Kent no longer felt clearly the difference between those insights arising on the inner or outer surface of his mental windshield.

You're Two Of A Kind, the newest billboard had read, And One Of You May Be Redundant. Kent found he couldn't agree more.

The sky was the color of a television tuned to the million dollar movie

Vantage and Strike mostly found that the more things were ruined the better they liked them. Perhaps the destruction enunciated something lurking in the things themselves at the outset, but Vantage and Strike could never have bothered with this perception: they were too deep inside the fact of the city to parse it as a concept, or to figure any possible alternative. The city was their natural world. Perhaps it was their irritation at the possibility of anything preceding the city that motivated their urge to shift it more deeply into a state of randomness, of an entropy to echo cosmic ruin. In any event, their tools were cruder than those of Salem and Marlboro, and their results more utterly violent. Vantage and Strike worked with spraycans and crowbars, with pots of unstable home-brewed acid concoctions and fecal smearings, but this was only because blowtorches, bullets and bombs were not available to them. They worked not in silence but with screams of laughter. The things they did to the billboards sometimes rendered whole zones unstable, and certainly struck fear in passersby. Yet they too were in a kind of conversation with the ancient marketing voices. They'd heard them their whole lives and in many senses could be seen as the children of those voices.

Vantage and Strike also attacked Salem and Marlboro's results, with gusto and glee equal to that with which they set themselves against the unaltered originals. That other presences labored at the billboards only exhilarated the younger men, but the solidarity they felt hardly precluded destruction of the older artists' works. This defacing was another conversation, a sign of life worth itself, no matter what might be obliterated in the meantime. The city around them, after all, burned. Here it was always night, and gangs roved the suburbs. More cars lay on their back or sides than not. Vantage and Strike didn't have the luxury of Salem and Marlboro's sunburnt vacancies, nor Kent's population-choked ennui. They wouldn't have known what to do if they had.

For you have it your way we do it all

Perhaps inevitable, Salem and Marlboro could envision an end to their work, not because it had failed, but because its success reframed not only the wasted city but their own vision of their places in it. They grew in different directions, until it was evident their partnership might begin slipping from them, ungrudgingly, in the manner of the desert's and the sky's widening influence. Salem had become compelled by these dawning blank spaces, the sand and sky, and so he began to contemplate billboards along vast lines, billboards to replace the sky or wrap around it, frames the viewer might be tempted to enter in and be lost. Salem contemplated the commercial power of natural history itself, the sales job implicit in Darwin's theory, each creature a refurbished model outmoding the previous on the showroom floor, the sun's irresistible advertisement for growth and mutation.

Marlboro went the other way, to the billboard as microcosm. It seemed to him that cars flashed their own little emblems and ads, the hubcaps, hood ornaments and particularly license plates, and so Marlboro began subtly altering these last, beginning with the coastal state's vanishing moniker: Call I'll Phone Ya, Kill For Nada, Car Porn Trivia. Clothing and eyewear, too, turned out when you looked to be riddled with tiny billboards, minute invasions of commerce into the subliminal life of the body. Even with eyes closed, flashbulb phosphenes burned into vision's screen by an unsetting sun might consist of a medium, one far beyond Madison Avenue's wildest dreams. Marlboro began scheming on this virgin re(tin)al estate, plotting to erect the first billboard of the inner eyelid.

Unkind donuts

Kent, still in his car, began unexpectedly dreaming of his apartment. In its architectural lineaments the place was a marvelous specimen, a 66th-level floor-through with picture panes on four sides, which had once featured panoramic views of ocean at one hand and mountains on the other, while downtown's spiny tangle unfolded vertiginously below. The last time he'd been there, however, Kent had noticed that obscenely huge and towering billboards had crept both higher and nearer to the apartment's windows, though he'd once been guaranteed that by signing the lease he'd decisively risen beyond their reach. Now, in his dreams, the apartment had expanded, its floor extending on all sides from his tiny oasis of furnishings as if it were in fact the surface of an abandoned planet or moon, while the walls had dropped away, leaving him starkly surrounded on all sides by the tremendous billboards. These had now become the functional walls of his apartment, and yet as familiar as this should have made the billboards, he found himself enthralled with their unexpectedly overripe color, their fractal complexity, and, though this should have been impossible due to the static nature of the medium, their absorbing narrative implications, which seemed richer by far than the events of his own daily existence. In fact, Kent couldn't take his eyes off them. Somehow this came as no surprise.

Chew bubblegum and kick ass at the same time

Vantage and Strike, digging in an alley's refuse to make a nest for sleeping off their latest bender, found to their surprise a cardboard box full of apparently unused sunglasses. The box, though buried beneath mounds of rubbish, seemed placed carefully, as though hidden. Sunglasses, however, were hardly an object of particular value in a city ruled by eternal night and regular power failures, one so frequently lit only by the flares of burning vehicles.

Yet Vantage and Strike were curious, and tried the glasses on. The result was revelatory, or consisted of hallucination disguised as revelation, or else in some manner illuminated the zone where the distinction between hallucination and revelation broke down permanently, or at least as long as one wore the glasses. The sunglasses seemed to render the world transparent of disguises. Businessmen were revealed, for the most part, as lizards, surprising no one. Commercial media exposed itself as a set of mind controls, as barren and direct as commands to Eat, Consume, Obey, Reproduce, and Remain Asleep. Yawn. The most fascinating, for Vantage and Strike, were the billboards: those they'd altered, and those they'd not yet reached, the ones on mile-high stilts or fenced-in by armed sentry-towers. They showed pictures, more vivid than the world itself, of the city sprawled and stretched in blazing noon, the streets empty apart from a few crouched figures or fugitive market stalls, the desert gaping between buildings that had once stood side by side. Then again they revealed the endless traffic jam, a huddled nightmare of smog and population. The billboards had become the last opportunity for the concurrent cities to sense one another: that one bereft in solar flares, the other choked with occupants straining to unreachable off ramps, this one savagely wrecked in moonshade. The divergence of the three was a lie, or so the sunglasses and the billboards seemed to claim.

Vantage and Strike each poked out one lens, so they could observe their city all ways at once, reality, dream and illusion in strobe simultaneity, a trick that quit giving them pounding headaches just a few days after they first tried it. No doubt this was not the use the glasses' manufacturer had intended, but the view was fucking outstanding that way.

Jonathan Lethem's eighth novel, *Chronic City*, was published in 2009. His others have been translated into nearly thirty languages. He lives in Maine and Brooklyn, New York.

Jim Greenhalf

Nichtomorph

When the cleverest intelligences
proclaim that the secret of the universe
is nothing but randomness,
what is the point of poetry or verse?

If *nothing* is a la carte,
enter a children's cancer ward;
tell them, tell their parents,
tell their friends,
the hope they feed on is aberrant.

I lost my way,
lost all sense of myself;
in the midnight hour,
at the mid-point of day.
So I settled for this nothing shape.

Now I am back
on the yellow brick road
with my unholy trinity of fools:
a fearful lion heart,
a thin-skinned man of tin,
a child of straw;
tendering my quest
for courage, hope and love,
in the magical land of
somewhere.

Gore Vidal at Hay-on-Wye

Holding court at the festival:
the old queen of a bygone age.
Instead of a throne a wheelchair.
Disdainful marble pillar
of cracks and wrinkles.

Once the respect was genuine;
now self-deprecation
is a necessary defence
against flattery
and ignorance.

It happens to all public figures
who outlive their achievements or,
like Hans Christian Anderson,
outstay their welcome.
Their very presence an unspoken rebuke.

The longing to be gone:
dust trapped in sunlight,
warmth thought but not felt;
the mind, ever conscious of itself,
never at rest nor peace.

Mars

We went to Mars
and fucked it up;
We left sad, soiled earth,

having sucked
the sweet blue planet dry.
That's why we went to the red one.

We exploited its arroyos
and scarred its scarlet heights.
And when we were done,

we set our sights on eight others
ours to ruin, before the sun
implodes and our solar light

diminishes to a spark.
But if, on the way,
our immune system collapses

and we roll around in faeces,
the capsule will merely be
like the hospitals we wrecked,

before we catapulted
the virus of this civilisation
between the Pillars of Creation.

Since his last publication in *Ambit*, Jim Greenhalf, in between public scandals, has
been working on his next collection. Given the stink emanting from Parliament, he
was toying with titles – *Ordure! Ordure!* perhaps, or *Mumpers*, a good old East End
term and a play on Tom Stoppard's stage play *Jumpers*. In fact, he has called it *The
Man in the Mirror* – with a message from the Poet Laureate.

Myra Schneider

Caffè Nero

Watching the juice whirled with ice to froth
then crowned with a transparent dome,
a pleasure dome that hypnotizes light
and invites fingers to stroke, sitting in the easy
air-conditioned cool sucking mango liquid
through a straw black as expresso coffee,
your thoughts crumpling as if they were tissues,
is to taste paradise. Looking through a glass
not darkly but clearly, you alight on the palace
of the Bishop of Winchester, a shell cross-hatched
by scaffolding and hemmed in by a warehouse,
the stone tracery of its rose window still intact.
Gazing through another glass expanse
you're surprised by the *Golden Hind*,
a replica bristling with decks and masts
and more alive than the beige skyscraper
across the slice of Thames. You remember
that just upriver the new Globe promises
an hour or so of Shakespeare experience
and now you expect to see Cleopatra sitting
in a burnished barge, purple sails flying –
but she's not on the water, she's by a doorway
talking on her mobile. In her lime trouser suit,
stunning against her olive skin, she stands tall
above the Saturday throng on the waterfront,
people like you who have left at home
the realities they find too hard to bear –
people in over-short shorts, magenta saris,
t-shirts strained over lumpy stomachs,
ice-cream lickers with wires in their ears, smilers
with prams, dogs – that dog, teeth into the lead
its owner's holding, lifted a foot off the ground.
And this heat, this cram, this jostle of London
is incongruous as your self – as all selves.
And though you could weep at your own,
at the world's bagfuls of unresolvables,
sitting with that pleasure dome of juice
in the café's cool on this last of June,
you are suddenly jubilant to be alive.

Running

He's dipping a red umbrella
into grass skinny as himself,
grass that's already flopping, grass
pale as his face, his coat, your thoughts.

The fumble of age in his step –
or is he blind? No, he's away
in his grey gaberdine, darting,
dotting. Not a shadow of doubt –

he's been let loose from lifeless rooms,
is a boy running and roughing
in fields he's not smelt for decades.
Or is it you who's running out

to breathe in cow-warmth, you haring
from a devil about to hurl
a stone? Quick! to the brook, gym shoes
sinking into mud and marsh gold…

The small zigzags come to a stop
and he turns. You have a vision
not of a foolish Lear but one
whose face is lit up with sheer joy.

And all that day you see nothing
but white grass that's wilting, wild hair,
a scarlet umbrella pointing,
all day you're smote by happiness.

Losing

Every sock in the bunch you're holding
is a dangling single. You wonder how many more
must be mouldering, partnerless, stuck in drawers.

Later, on the way to work, you remember
the lost mug patterned with rosemary you think
an absent-minded friend slipped into her bag,

and picture the half-dead umbrella you left on a bus.
But all this is trivial on a day when the smudged air
is buzzing with the loss of jobs, self-respect, children.

Hopeless, you fold the newspaper, turn to now –
this moment on a train underground: that black lad,

beautiful in his pale blue anorak. You try to work out
why his hands are across his eyes. To block out
the world as he listens to the sounds wires
are bringing to his ears? To survey the carriage?

Already this now has passed out of reach, become
a memory which will sink or swim among millions
of others in your mind's measureless caverns.

Now, you visualize time as unstoppable sand falling
through a sieve, count the growing refusals
of your body. They remind you a moment will come

when you'll lose the privilege of consciousness,
remind you not to hang around limply as a sock
but to forestall this last loss with findings:

a sparrowhawk perched on your gate, eyes alert
for prey, words that toadleap from imagination,
from heart – to make sure every day is a finding.

Myra Schneider's most recent collection is *Circling The Core* (Enitharmon, 2008).
Writing Your Self, written with John Killick, is a key resource book of personal writing
and literature.

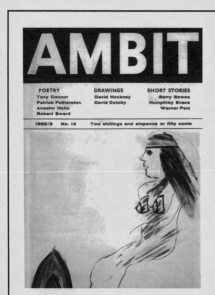

AMBIT No. 14
Ferguson was gone, but
in a good change Michael
Foreman appeared. They
met briefly and clearly
agreed with each other's
ideas. The cover needed a
strong image, so Foreman
first produced a Peter
Blake for issue 13, and
then this Hockney drawing
for Ambit 14.

Bible Story 4 – The Genesis Sequence

This is a Martin Bax and Robert MacAulay Bible story. These stories, which have appeared since *Ambit* 154, reverse the usual sequence of events in the magazine's production. Usually artists are presented with text to illustrate. With Bible Stories Mac presents Martin with seven or eight images and Martin has to respond with text. For the first one Martin linked the images with a Bible story. He has continued to do so, although Robert makes no concessions to this approach with the diversity of his artwork.

God: Let there be light.

And there was light.

Root Toot: Well done old fellow. I was looking for the switch, but you've done the trick for me. Congratulations on your Creation business. Martin said we should meet up because I'm in the creation business too. See this saxophone of mine? A real little beaut. I made it myself and they're selling all over town. Helped with rent a bit… But what do you get up to?

God: In the beginning I created the Heaven and Earth. And the Earth was without form, and void. And my Spirit moved upon the face of the…

Root Toot: Well it all sounds a bit formulaic to me. But I recognise your text now: it's out of the old Bibel. I shall have a look at it and see whether I can sort things out a bit. Maybe we could do a bit together.

God: And I saw the light and it was good: and I divided the light from the darkness. I called the light Day, and the darkness I called Night.

Root Toot: What's your first name then – I think you and I should get beyond surnames. My friends call me Rootie. What about you? Go go! Well any rate I'm in different creations to you. I'm into the music itself.

God: And the evening and the morning were the first day.

God: I made the firmament, and divided the waters which were under the firmament from the waters which were above the firmament: and it was so.

And I called the firmament Heaven.

Root Toot: Heaven! I'm in Heaven when we're dancing cheek to cheek. Hey God, but I'm going to jump you about a bit here. I mean, I want the lady, and nobody's having one of my ribs. I'll want all my ribs intact when I get going. With this chick you call her Eve and she surely looks good. I want her out of that bath.

God: It is not good that the man should be alone; I will make him a help meet for him. And I caused a deep sleep to fall upon Adam, and he slept: and I took one of his ribs, and closed up the flesh instead thereof; And the rib, which I had taken from man, made I a woman, and brought her unto the man.

Root Toot: Naughty naughty!

God: Therefore shall a man leave his father and his mother, and shall cleave unto his wife: and they shall be one flesh. And they were both naked, the man and his wife, and were not ashamed.

Root Toot: They were having it off of course, you're a bit naive Goddy. If you think that boys don't find out early on in their lives what you can get up to in gardens.

God: And Adam knew Eve his wife; and she conceived, and bore Cain, and said, I have gotten a man from the Lord.

Root Toot: Hang on Goddy, what's going on here? Were you having it off with Eve? I don't like the sound of that; I want Eve all to myself and right now I'm getting her out of the bath. But I'm reckoning to stay in your Garden of Eden. Forget the serpents.

God: And the evening and the morning were the second day.

God: Let the earth bring forth grass, the herb yielding seeds, and the fruit tree yielding fruit after his kind, whose seed is in itself.

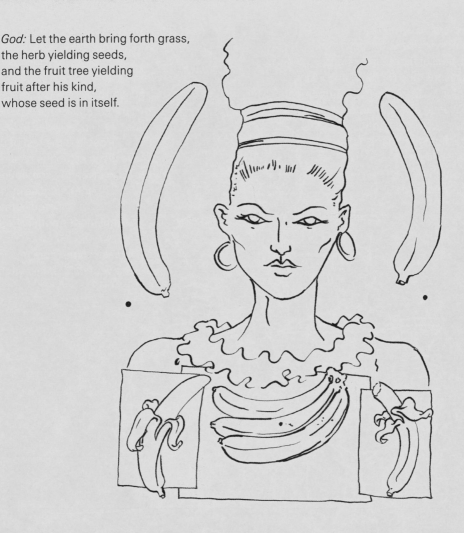

Root Toot: I've always liked bananas because as a little boy we couldn't get them. But what about you, Goddy? Here we are in the middle of Eden and I don't reckon when you were playing around in Eden you had bananas. They came from the Carribean, after Eden. Best get your facts straight, Goddy.

God: Abel was a keeper of sheep, but Cain was a tiller of the ground. And in process of time it came to pass, that Cain brought of the fruit of the ground an offering unto me. And Abel, he also brought of the firstlings of his flock and of the fat thereof.

Root Toot: Hang on, Goddy, this is getting nasty.

God: I had respect unto Abel and his offering, but unto Cain and his offering I had no respect.

Root Toot: It's what happens to my music, nobody likes it but I still play it. And I've got my own group now and we're generally creative, but get the Beeb to play me? Forget it. Perrhaps you could help me Goddy.

God: Am I my brother's keeper?

Root Toot: When can I have a banana again?

God: And the evening and the morning were the third day.

God: Let there be lights in the firmament of the heaven to divide the day from the night; and let them be for signs, and for seasons, and for days, and years: And let them be for lights in the firmament of the heaven to give light upon the earth. And I made two great lights; the greater light to rule the day, and the lesser light to rule the night: I made the stars also.

.

Root Toot: Day four and the newspapers have got hold of it. Well, bound to happen wasn't it. What's more I think you'll like it. I guess you've always wanted to be famous and your old Babel has been superceded at last. Trouble is the rest of us have given up on the papers. I m busy inventing something that reduces news at a regular rate until there's nothing left.

I'll make some more music. I've just invented Shostakovitch.

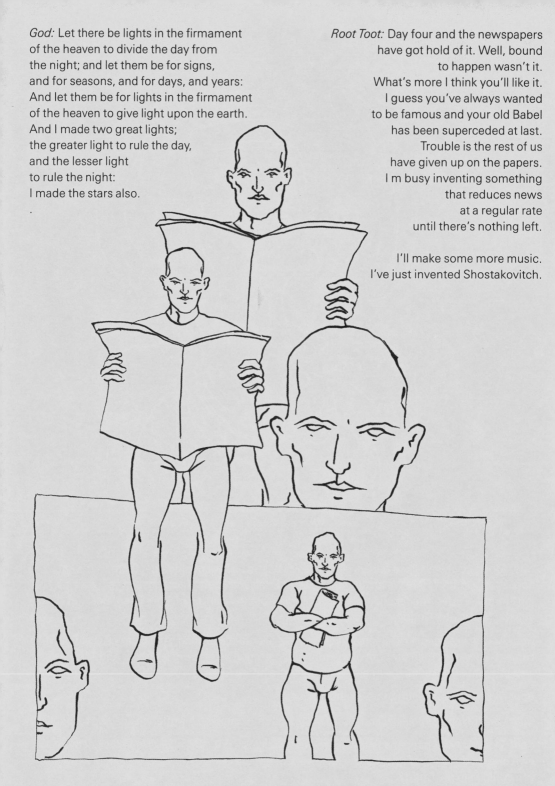

God: And the evening and the morning were the fourth day

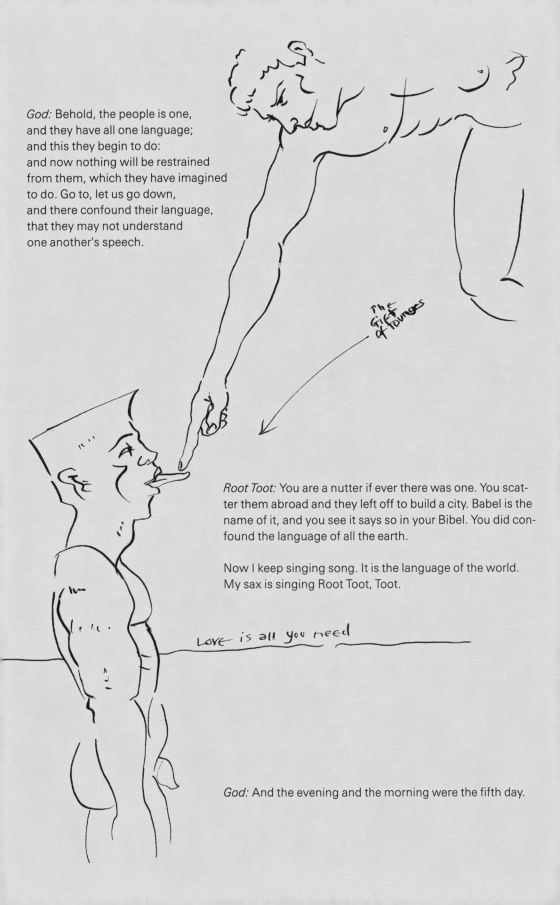

God: Behold, the people is one, and they have all one language; and this they begin to do: and now nothing will be restrained from them, which they have imagined to do. Go to, let us go down, and there confound their language, that they may not understand one another's speech.

Root Toot: You are a nutter if ever there was one. You scatter them abroad and they left off to build a city. Babel is the name of it, and you see it says so in your Bibel. You did confound the language of all the earth.

Now I keep singing song. It is the language of the world. My sax is singing Root Toot, Toot.

God: And the evening and the morning were the fifth day.

God: What hast thou done? The voice of thy brother's blood crieth unto me from the ground. And now art thou cursed from the earth, which hath opened her mouth to receive thy brother's blood from thy hand; When thou tillest the ground, it shall not henceforth yield unto thee her strength; a fugitive and a vagabond shalt thou be in the earth.

Root Toot: Clubbing always leads to trouble? I keep clear of it myself. You see a bastard like this one kicking a bin you know he's only got mischief on his mind. So what do you do. Into the motor and out of it. Saturday nights, well they do end on Sunday.

God: And the evening and the morning were the sixth day.

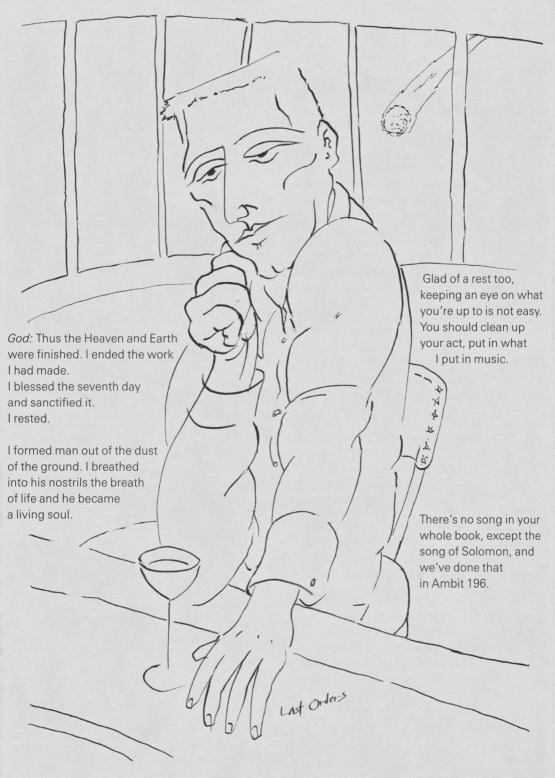

God: Thus the Heaven and Earth were finished. I ended the work I had made.
I blessed the seventh day and sanctified it.
I rested.

I formed man out of the dust of the ground. I breathed into his nostrils the breath of life and he became a living soul.

Glad of a rest too, keeping an eye on what you're up to is not easy. You should clean up your act, put in what I put in music.

There's no song in your whole book, except the song of Solomon, and we've done that in Ambit 196.

Last Orders

Root Toot: Now I'll blow away even as you rest, and Root Toot-Toot. Yes, I will take a glass of wine. I hope it's not one you created. Bye bye God.

God: And the evening and the morning were the seventh day.

Carole Satyamurti

Night Train to Bologna

Go because you have the freedom not to.
You've seen so many beautiful cities
they blur like old smoke,
but because those cities are never truly lost,
take the night train to Bologna.

Go for the idea of it – night
a lava-flow through fields, down streets
of silent boxes whose lids protect, conceal.
You've chosen enigma, this transposition
in the no time that is sleep,

chosen to risk the embarrassment of sleep
with strangers, to test what can be trusted,
what can be borne.
Nothing simpler than lying down to sleep,
nothing more at the mercy.

Go for the merciful escape,
to find your different
tongue, more vivacious
and more halting – go
to know the foolishness of being foreign.

Know you must record this, now –
that soon, the yet to come that is Bologna
will clutter up with fact and memory.
Travelling on this night train
will never taste the same again

though if you get a taste for it, hooked
on lightness, then you'll take
the night train for Trieste, Kazan,
Novosibirsk…each name more open
than the last; each to be realised, and left.

The Sunday Fathers

You see them in parks,
McDonald's, shopping centres,
neatly pressed children,
well-shaven fathers:
Happy Families with the Mrs missing;
she's a gap in the afternoon.

They watch each other
without seeming to.
Where does the father go
when he's not with them?
They can't imagine him.
They worry without words.

What can the fathers ask?
And how? They don't remember
the names of best friends, teachers.
Did they before? Have they
always got the wrong things right?

They eke the questions out
like spending money.
They try – how they try!
By evening, all of them are bleak,
exhausted.

It's heartbreak by a thousand monosyllables,
a thinning of the skeleton of love
until it snaps.

Carole Satyamurti's most recent collection is *Stitching the Dark: New and Selected Poems* (Bloodaxe, 2005). She is currently working on a new English version of the Mahabharata.

The Modernist Uprising

H. P. Tinker

You dead ones – I lay with you under the unbroken wires…
Ivor Gurney, 'Farewell'

Today I glimpsed Esther Williams riding a unicycle through Bloomsbury, dressed in the glorious raggle-taggle gypsy apparel of the wayward daughter of the Lord of Bostick. I gazed at her for several seconds half-transfixed, quasi-perplexed, semi-tantalised by her kerchiefed head, tattered petticoat, bare legs, vagabond sandals …between stiff doses of Benzedrine and tales of her savage Apache lovers, we talked of memory and truth and observed the polite etiquette of consuming good salad.

'You eviscerated lately?' she asked, between forkfuls.

'Yeah,' I admitted, knifing sub-zero lettuce. 'There have been some small moments of quiet evisceration.'

She drew in her legs and raised my eyebrows with an emphatic emphasis on the inclusiveness of the first-person plural.

'The struggle for life is exhausting!' she cried. 'This is a time of war! We are the fighters of the war! This, finally, is our war! Let's fight it then! Fight it and fight it and fight it some more with all the passion we have and all the resolve we can summon and/or muster…You see, a bit of action is required every now and again, and in a time of war action is so precious, especially to younger people with nothing to do…We must face our destiny shoulder to shoulder, you and I. Embrace the void. There is nothing to fear here anymore. The conflict shall be cathartic. We will force them to be free!'

Then she removed her dress to reveal a gleaming metallic bathing suit beneath.

'I may look like Henry James,' I told her, reaching for an electric can opener. *'But I feel more like Robert Frost…'*

Of all the 3000 girls of the uprising, she remained my favourite by far. As soon as she left, everything looked immediately bleak again. Like Walt Whitman's New York, George Gissing's London, Philip Larkin's Hull, this city was dying, frozen in the icy grip of the contemporary literary novel. I knocked on Wittgenstein's door. A former lawyer with extremely bad luck, he was encountering various difficulties with his significantly younger wife. Yet still he managed miscellaneous comic asides about Modernism, even mentioning the likelihood of a future uprising…

'It may well prove a fine example of generational revolt against ascendant liberalism and hegemonic conservatism,' he explained, 'but any future uprising should not be interpreted as absolutely oppositional in nature. All bourgeois art has become an escape, a refuge from the unpleasant world of increasingly threatening political reality, culturally compelling, gargantuan construction, monumental manifestations. This new generation has no alternative but to seek the sympathy and support of an older generation inclined to take an interest in literary and artistic developments. Like the intimate correlation of a dysfunctional family, the Oedipally rebellious sons depend on the abusive patronage of elderly paternal institutions and an ambivalent maternal public…'

Wittgenstein spoke with the apocalyptic fervour of a sixteenth-century court jester receiving medication.

'What is this conversation about?' I asked myself later.

Time-rich, I telephoned Hilda Doolittle, a beautiful but emotionally fragile spy rumoured to be a former bookshop owner.

'Do you remember a similar time when we were young and the world was a much sunnier place?' I asked.

'No,' she hissed.

Where clerks and aristocrats had previously failed, I rebuked her with the words: 'Tandis que je suis, moi, à bûcher comme un nègre, vous vous repassez du bon temps…'

She fluttered her false eyelashes down the line and hung up.

Cash-penniless, I decided to go outside, disguise myself as an artist, see what was going down in China Town. Nothing much, it transpired. So, pasting a grossly exaggerated flannelette goatee onto my chin with a beeswax-based adhesive, strapping on a prosthetic penis, as a precaution, I entered the semi-dark indifference of a bourgeois lounge bar decorated in the appalling semi-dark indifferent style of a bourgeois lounge bar. As I was wearing my frayed nineteenth-century coat, ruffled vest and extravagant silk cravat, I passed unnoticed amidst the tangled ephemera of earnest aesthetes in velvet jackets, stern lesbians in pinstripe suits, male models in monocles, kohl-eyed beauties adorned by chiffon and beads and feathers and emeralds. Many fallen bohemians had taken refuge here, happy, it seemed, to take their chances amongst the financially diseased, the sexually bankrupt, the sartorially dispossessed, and Wallace Stevens. I spent much of the evening drinking contaminated burgundy with W. H. Auden, discussing Freytag's Triangle, Krafft-Ebing, mutual masturbation and Proust.

'I've recently noticed that my memories are peculiarly Proustian,' Auden confessed. 'They nearly always take me back to another time and place where my younger self was previously present…'

I ate my hat and showed myself out.

You came to me then, cool and flower-like at the zebra crossing. You smelt of Carthage. A Prozac addict, obsessed with cleanliness, your conversations revolved around disease and the inevitable deterioration of all human home furnishings. Among the behemoths, we sat in adjacent deckchairs and drank tall white coffee, surrounded by unholy saints and scholars. 'What do you want from the future?' you asked. 'Are creativity and cookery truly compatible? What is the real purpose of city breaks? How can you entertain yourself without money? Is it necessary to stay sober? Is any of it worth it in the end? How can you live beautifully and cheaply? Do you really need furniture? What is the point of wallpaper? Must women wear skirts? Is jewellery ever right on a man? Must men be clean-shaven? What does an artist do when they run out of money? Is homosexuality wrong? Is marriage meaningful? What is wrong with sex outside marriage anyway? Is there such a thing as free love? Does humanity have a function in the universe? Why is poverty so romantic? How can you survive producing something nobody wants? And do so with good grace and self-contained interior mental resilience?'

I jumped to my own defence.

'The price of freedom is poverty,' I admitted. 'But although I am always starving, I never actually starve…'

You banged my head tenderly, many times, and told me to shut up and sit down and stand up for myself. (NOTE. It was you, then, who I turned to during the intermediate phase of my struggle for personal freedom. You drew me a map to your door and I grabbed my passport, caught a slow train, and travelled to Vienna where the scenery changed around me. I buried my feelings there — all 18 of them — and dared you to follow.

Instead, April came.

And still I waited for you to come.

Then May came.

And still I waited for you to come.

Soon after, I found myself embracing June wholeheartedly. *And still I waited for you to come*. When June found out about April-Louise and Betty May she slapped me in the face and I never heard from her again. Once I had condemned Viva King for having an illegal relationship with a blind priest named Igor who had been disfigured in a house fire.

Now I realised she had been perfectly within her rights.

It was in Vienna, as I lay — *still waiting for you to come* — that I was overtaken by a rare moment of weakness. I took off my clothes and climbed on top of Betty May again. A dirty porn star with dwarfism, after a period in the Prussian army and posing as a drapery assistant for Jacob Epstein, Betty May had become a cocaine enthusiast, converted to Roman Catholicism, and was currently working as a PA for Aleister Crowley. Having made my hasty ascent to the uppermost peak of her highest pinnacles, the moment passed more swiftly than I had anticipated and I was left up there, stranded, feeling faintly foolish.

She ordered me to climb off and sit in a corner.

I waited there in warm silence, a kind of liquid running between both buttocks. Under duress, I admitted that my name was Hugo von Hofmannsthal and that I was secretly an underground novelist, librettist, poet, dramatist, and essayist. Other memories and thoughts flowed into my mind, a visit to Oscar Peterson's speakeasy with Max Reinhardt, and Arthur Schnitzler's strange encounter with Iris Tree in Leningrad.

I wondered to whom these memories originally belonged.

Betty May departed to appear in an all-nude production of *Summer Holiday* and was knighted for services to nudity. She eventually moved to Cornwall, became an opiate gardener and shot herself. She survived but became over-fashionable in Paris where she succumbed to sex addiction and contractual disappointments. Then she fell from the Eiffel tower restaurant and strangled herself in her own scarf after it became entangled in the wheels of the oncoming ambulance. Alone, in corridors of gold and blue, I wept, briefly…*and still I waited for you to come.*)

You never came, of course. Had my penis not been quite so putrid and foul-smelling, perhaps you might have found me irresistible…

May 11. Back in the hubris of the city, I heard talk of the new Modernist movement. There were social rumblings underfoot, like ideological indigestion. The old regime was cracking and crumbling; akin to the very flags of pavement I was standing on, the fractures were severe. An imbalance of bohemianism and big business held the city in a magical thrall precipitating a hostage-situation in the form of young, idealistic balladeers, leather caps in hand. I found them lurking in the underground attics of crowded pop cafés where I grew amused by the over-arching earnestness of the new generation, cabaret singers mostly, who expressed themselves in decadent and melancholic verse attuned to a sense of collective Oedipal revolt:

'There is a discreet
But very tender
Sense of symbiosis
Now in operation'

sang one small child who had only begun writing cabaret songs at the turn of the century. Indeed he wore a wide-brimmed moustache to disguise his acute naivety. I realised he was warning of a strange time to come when even slightly annoying people who had previously failed badly would rise up from their sofa beds and achieve some kind of unwarranted success…

I spent the next three months in the Café Royale, sharing coffee and narcotics with Enid Bagnold and Tom Petty, formerly of The Heartbreakers. We could hear modernism rising from our gravy and mashed potatoes in an audible sound slightly reminiscent of Dvořák. How I survived during this period I am not certain. I had only a small attic room at L'Apartments Rue Morgue, near Queer Street, and made a meagre living painting indifferent watercolours for the local rappers and drug dealers. My room was furnished sparsely, the empty sense of my own worthlessness punctuated by busts of Wagner and Beethoven, owl effigies, ivory Buddhas, Chinese fertility goddesses, small Greek gods of gold, silver, brass, iron, wood, plastic, stone and colour pictures of wild daisies torn out of Sunday supplements. This period passed largely without incident. Then, one morning, from outside came a loud thud, smack, belch. I realised it was Virginia Woolf and opened the door immediately. We exchanged good-natured banter, the word 'bugger' never far from her lips. Then, suddenly dramatic and overtly tomboyish, she came flying at me with a razor blade, threatening to write a sequel to *Mrs Dalloway*.

I saw at once she was deadly serious.

We glared at one another, neither daring to blink.

Eventually it grew dark and she left down the fire escape.

The next day I woke to a sound not unlike elliptical gunfire.

A cock was crowing rowdily on a rooftop and the city below was in a bit of a fever. The entire metropolis was under concerted attack from a pan-generational troupe of sequined belly dancers prancing in the late style of Isadora Duncan. Some gallant Arabs detonated themselves dutifully. The streets were quickly barricaded with protective copper wire, the perimeters patrolled by pimps, wastrels, vagabonds, gypsies, actors, prostitutes, thieves, beekeepers, filmmakers, picture-house pianists, watchmakers and a one-armed chef.

After breakfast, I read in the *Morning Star* that the terrible forces of embourgeoisement had swept into the East, pursued hotly by the deafening sound of Fidel Castro's brother reciting the *Iliad*. Meanwhile, the Midday News reported that a consortium of hirsute guitar wizards was defecating on Primrose Hill. Then I learned from the *Evening Standard* that a group of radical poets were reading Spinoza by candlelight and abstaining from shaving. Excited by the prospect of my own undeserved success, I could not sleep. Wearing a pair of the tightest underpants known to man, I sought out these radicals, discovered them gathered beneath the colossal inflatable

beard of Karl Marx: Guillaume, Albert, Brett, Iris, Jean, Ginger, Walter, Kurt and Basil, bright young people, impossibly languid, lazing amidst the crazy pavements and skewed Doric towers. Huddled together they masturbated quietly, deep into the following afternoon. I was disappointed by their tremendous ordinariness and became confused and as I attempted to leave was struck from behind by a copy of Simulacra and Simulation, hurled at distance, with much precision...

I came round in a scholarly office suffused with the scintillating scent of stale mint tea. I glanced up to see Pierre Reverdy wearing a gold lamé suit, engaged in the difficult process of sprinkling brown sugar over his bacon. The walls were faded and pink academic papers piled up ceiling-high, dusty and apparently unthumbed. A stringless cello sat alone in a corner.

'You wanted to see me,' said Pierre, not looking up.

'Not really,' I said.

He threatened me with a warm embrace.

I shook him by the arm instead.

Although his face had been skin-jetted recently, beneath his Beatnik facial hair lay a craggy, visionary poet who had learnt the secrets of love and art and war and then forgotten them again.

'Oh, it's all true,' he said, still not quite looking up. 'I am one of the very earliest founding Beatniks. My short verse never received the same recognition as other later Beatniks, largely because it was so good. Now I am very old. I have spent 70 years mixing the poetic with the domestic in my search for the truth — and so far I have yet to find out anything very specific. I fear it is too late to tell you of my many failed attempts at falling in love and becoming world famous disguised as Ezra Pound. I think I was trying to subvert the entire Corporate Universe, trying to create a whole new Empire... unfortunately, it never quite happened...'

Pierre then began arguing about the increasing power of the 'object' over the 'subject' in modern society. Blood dribbled out of my nostrils. When I regained my senses he was giving a grand account of the last siege of Paris: '...with the last revolution ending so badly things just weren't the same. The timbre of the times was different, new post-war days where it seemed that unbeknownst to me much of modern culture contained an alarming course of visceral indoctrination...'

After a number of gratuitous meetings in strip clubs, I eventually believed in the cause and signed some papers and was issued with my own battalion comprising a bisexual army deserter, a damaged ex-Spitfire pilot, a young Arabian rentboy, a French transsexual prostitute, a clumsy American college girl, a best-selling Egyptian writer left blinded from an operation and suffering from an acute mental illness because his child was stolen by childless bandits after his wife left him for a much less well-endowed man, and my former gay flatmate, Gustav. Two weeks later, to Gustav's and everybody else's surprise, the uprising began.

In the northern district, a heavy bombardment of angry penguins fizzed snakily through the streets. Captain Yates gave the signal with his tin whistle and we ran, as quickly as we could, in the opposing direction, across relentless plains of cement, beneath falling towers, the city bursting into scalding fragments and burning ruins like a cracking Bartok cacophony. Back at base, we cordoned off Phil Spector's hair and inoculated all surviving modern artists against various vacuous strains of Cuban cubism. Then we tied young Merrick to a lamppost, his grotesque, bulbous appearance frightening the frontline of nervous young women.

Captain Yates asked, 'What is he doing there?'

'He has been usually blue of late, sir,' I explained. 'He needs some restraint in his life.'

An out-of-work narrator approached and reported that the first wave of children's authors had been repulsed from the rear by a team of monks, bloggers, and scantily-clad showgirls. Yet many more were coming from other directions. On the horizon, an army of glamorous businesswomen appeared dancing alongside gigantic golden coins, using Nelly Furtado's bisexuality as a cynical marketing ploy. Wittgenstein fired a salvo of ball bearings over their heads. Yeowling *rat-a-tat-tat* into a sudden **BLAST!** the afternoon exploded into a joyful kind of inane apocalypse. The women tumbled. Many began to sob uncontrollably; others were overcome by fitful fits, giggling, guffawing, the furious sound of a laughter epidemic. We were pelted with rotten apples and Ivor Gurney fell, wounded, gassed, most probably shell-shocked or at the very least half-drunk. The Oedipal Light Infantry sank to their kneepads, sobbing at the feet of Ida Nettleship.

In the confusion, I set a big chair on fire.

Somehow we muddled on until morning. Amidst the thick cigar smoke, it was difficult to tell what had happened, why it had happened, or who had won, but all the worst passages of violence seemed to be over. I had wounds on my arms and resignation over my face. I kicked down Wittgenstein's door and he greeted me tersely. He had been watching the whole thing through binoculars from his loft conversion.

'The uprising has failed fairly badly,' he told me.

'Yes, I guessed as much,' I said. 'Will there be other uprisings?'

'Most likely,' said Wittgenstein. 'Uprisings come and go quite frequently these days. Though unsuccessful, this uprising will ultimately pave the way for a second uprising and then a third and then a fourth.'

'*And then?*'

'Very likely a fifth.'

I sat down on a gloomy leather sofa and aged, experiencing broken-hearted existentialism until late into the afternoon. How my feelings at that moment were exacting, exigent, like a late-night stabbing in an artificial leg…

The coldness of war soon giving way to a grey new world of utility. As a warning, Vita Sackville-West was hoisted onto a plinth and paraded in a spinning birdcage. Many disillusioned survivors lined the graveside of Gertrude Stein to watch Noam Chomsky's fantastic firework display. Overhead the stars had vacated the sky, the faceless moon was fading and several men who couldn't grow full beards were lurking in artistic berets, beside bodegas. Next to me, a smiling poet in a tuxedo was carrying the bleeding heart of Ern Malley.

'The day of my eventual death,' announced Gertrude Stein from a marble lectern, 'will be a tremendously sad day for all of you…'

Over on the corner, a disturbance was threatening the commerce of polite society. Eschewing the elegant restraint of Mies van der Rohe in his prime, Richard Ellmann was making a rambling admission about the inadequacy of biography to get to the truth of any given situation and, having drunk too much Spanish wine, had picked a fight with Augustus John over the size of each other's biceps. Many similar conflicts remained unresolved, several involving my former landlady Mrs Equitone.[1] In this context of post-war austerity and rampant hedonism, I wrote Esther a letter.

Esther!

Time has drowned you in unfair obscurity! I think of you quite often. The uprising failed and as I write this, Rob Lowe's sadness hangs thick over the city, the steady accumulation of a small career blighted by massive misfortune. I remain immune to it all (having been vaccinated on the back of a Triumph motorcycle by Egon Schiele.) Esther! I heard you contracted incurable gonorrhoea from a 50s fairground operator and have become involved in the women's suffrage movement. Are you feeling better? Well, I remember what you once told me[2] and have subsequently come to realise you were absolutely right. Dear Esther! How is your disease today? Do not think harshly of me. I was caught in a tangled web but was not responsible for the majority of the weaving. I merely embroidered a little at the margins. When I removed myself from the situation it was due to swamps of middle-class realism, disorientated members of the upper classes, the low-dimensional topology of Thurston Moore's geometrization. Esther! I miss you! I do! But the feelings involved were too large and entangled and the death of language eventually occurred in a tiny village of naked gardeners, soulful beekeepers. I thought I was at my lowest ebb there, in the village, but soon discovered there were other, even lower ebbs. In fact, there seemed no end to the depths an ebb could lower itself. Modernism had been my future, you see, but perhaps it is time to begin again. Now that the past is gone, I have eschewed domestic violence and begun exchanging letters with a filthy woman named Martha, who lives near Copenhagen. Esther! Won't you come back to Bloomsbury? All the friends I ever had are gone. How I pray hourly for a new Modernist uprising of an entirely younger generation…

and that winter, brand new Modernists began arriving, dewy-eyed, malnourished, draped in raggedy rags like small hopeful Third World children. As I lay bedridden, paranoiac, underwhelmed by the unprecedented idiosyncrasies of the new metropolis, precocious cultural modernism was being openly touted by effete students in cafés and paraded by bearded professors in bandanas. Just as I had completely lost the ability to speak or write or think of anything coherently, down in the working-class streets, the controversial theme of sexual deviance permeated a landscape largely being held together by wishful thinking: Tim Robbins was completely exonerated, Slobodan Milosevic joined a rejuvenated Take That and the reconstruction of Will Self's ego began in earnest. Mean American memes flourished alongside other kinds of permissiveness: silly symphonies, risible harmonies, gloopy yellow sound…I put on a natty trilby and married Mrs Equitone, that fine-looking divorcee with most of her own teeth still

1. A fine-looking divorcee with most of her own teeth intact.
2. 'The struggle for life is exhausting! This is a time of war! We are the fighters of the war! This, finally, is our war! Let's fight it then! Fight it and fight it and fight it some more with all with all the passion we have and all the resolve we can summon and/or muster…you see, a bit of action is required every now and again, and in a time of war, action is so precious, especially to younger people with nothing to do…we must face our destiny shoulder to shoulder, you and I. Embrace the void. There is nothing to fear here anymore. The conflict shall be cathartic. We will force them to be free!'

intact. Although many people immediately threw their hands up in horror and wept for me, I was determined to regard it as a happy ending.

Outside St Paul's, nothing but mouldy Edwardians pervaded the proceedings. After the quickest of ceremonies, Charles Pierre Baudelaire stood up and polemicised contemptuously against cars, Walter Gropius recited a rousing showtune about the marvellous breasts of Bavarian women, while Walt Whitman whistled random names and addresses from the telephone book.

'Which side are you on?' I asked Mrs Equitone, who had been drinking quite heavily since noon.

'Weialala leia,' she cried.

I spilled wine down my pants nine times in the course of the same evening.

'Weialala leia,' Mrs Equitone cried again, a little later, as we were about to consummate our married union for the first time. 'Wallala leialala.'

I plunged my fingers into my ears and thought of Bloomsbury.

A recent recipient of the Guggenheim MacArthur Genius Award, H. P. Tinker was first published in *Ambit* during the last century. J. D. Salinger called him 'the greatest contemporary short story writer living in Chorlton-cum-hardy today'. Harper Lee declined to comment. 'The Modernist Uprising' is an extract from a probably unpublishable work-in-progress, *Conspiracy of Eununchs*.

AMBIT

A stars and Stripes Special with Martin Bax, Gavin Ewart, Michael Foreman Giles Gordon getting in a few blows at the old U.S. image and then from th good old U.S.A. itself come Michael Benedikt, Marvin Cohen, Bob Kaufman John Keys, Gary Kissick, David Ray, Uncle Bob Sward et al.

| 1969 | Number 39 | Three shillings or two francs |

AMBIT No. 39
Ambit had attracted the attention of James Laughlin, editor of New Directions, and we decided on a special American number. It was the time of the Chicago riots, and Michael Foreman was by now solidly ensconced as Ambit's art editor. A complaint was lodged about the cover artwork, so a policeman called in at the Ambit offices. 'If only,' he said, 'it wasn't so well drawn.'

Vidyan Ravinthiran

Elegy

Bluish   soft   I am here
I am not lying   I appreciate
everything you've done a wilderness
of skyscrapers   I know the trapdoor
will not open stillwe have come so far you and I
each car rushing by is like
the surf   a moment of surf
the clock a deathwatch misses the point
Did I ever tell you your face
in the last moment was joyous I'm not lying
nothing is hard or soft enough anymore
there are no breasts   in the dead of night
listening to her toss and turn   dawn down
the lane   everything in me wants to run
there are colours and a tension in the broken slats
I am not finished Can you hear
the first birds tough it out   on wires and gables   hum
of the mini-fridgethe blinking light a strained device I'm sure
Durex in tissue paper   uncrumpling
beneath the wrecked mattress
like water-lilies by Monet   I could go on like this
a line of barbed wire bisects the hillside   dawncold
we are there again   I am sorry
the dead of night affords no breasts   did you hear that
something solid too solid must intervene
The dregs in the wineglass the taste in your head
I am not finished

Rambutan

Between the elephant orphanage at Dambulla
where, blinded years ago by hunters' shot, a huge tusker

kept mournfully stock-still as granite in the shade
while we caressed his rubbery, crosshatched, stiff-haired hide

and the spice garden where my parents, drugged with sugary herbal
tea pressed on them by our guide, accepted the magical

properties of unprocessed turmeric, we drove
a hundred miles or more though steamy palm-tree groves,

passed dozens of identical rickety stalls old hands
kept stocked with gaudy batiks and bananas, garlands

of postcards flashing the sunlight back at us, and bought
not a single one of those pyramid-heaped red fruit,

dusty balls with flexible prongs like some kind of Nerf ammunition
or a stress-relieving toy for executives – it seems rambutan

vendors replenish their displays constantly,
either that or no one ever buys any,

the dust on these tough red skins too rarely peeled back
by the callused thumbs that make it down this track

to expose the clear meat like an eyeball's you must learn
to scrape off with your teeth around its hard red stone.

Sigiriya

Kasyapa's neurotic fortress sits atop the ugly heart of a volcano
whose sun-baked clines and scree eroded aeons ago,
leaving only this big fuck-off monadnock like God's fist

banged down in the middle of nowhere. Plaster dust
seals lifelines shut and ruins
with more than thumbprint blur your zoom-in on the lion's paw

hewed of a man-high drip-shelf – there used to be two
but that fearful symmetry's vanished
where emissaries once kowtowed for admission through

the whole beast's intact jaws as at the MGM Grand before
the enforced taboos of oriental high-rollers. The mirror wall's immaculate
eggwhite and beeswax glaze is now grey chalk reflecting only heat.

Of the cloudmaidens fresco-painters repeated longingly
over the bare rock surfaces, only a few *apsaras* have survived
the iconoclasm of prudish monks to arch their swan-necks for the camera.

Their exaggerated breasts provoke
unanachronistically, if anything – bad poems dedicated to them
by wall-eyed courtiers get tagged over constantly with love-hearts

fletched with permanent marker, western txtspeak that aspires to Hebrew.

Vidyan Ravinthiran is a graduate student and lecturer at Balliol College, Oxford.
His pamphlet, *At Home or Nowhere*, was published in 2008 by tall lighthouse; other
poems have appeared in *Tower Poetry Review*, *Magma*, *Poetry Review*, *The North*,
and the *Times Literary Supplement*.

Charles Roff

Charlie's Angels

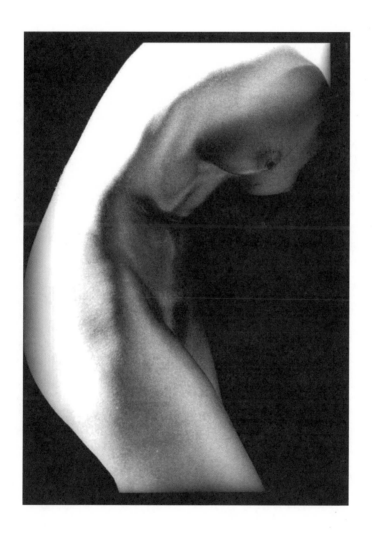

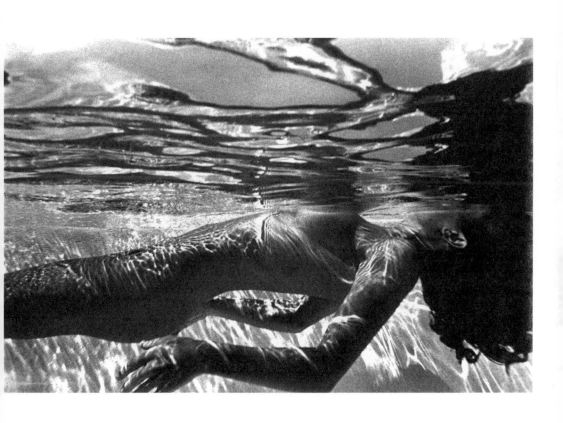

Fleur Adcock

Goodbye to New Zealand

What with getting in the way of the packing
and not being allowed to go to
the big event, Great-granny's funeral,

we found something silly to do, and did it:
we sat the new dolls on the potty
after we'd done wees in it ourselves.

Next day we were going away in a boat
so big that you could stand up in it,
they said, and it wouldn't tip over.

There was no time to dry the soggy dolls;
they were left behind – all but my Margaret,
who wouldn't bend enough to dunk her bottom.

Frant

Bliss cottage, in retrospect:
woods just across the road, a duckpond
in the field behind, cowslips...

even at the time we loved it.
Living in Sussex, going to school in Kent:
how travelled we sounded!

I had my eleventh birthday there:
books, and cake for tea in the back parlour
we rented from Mrs Gain.

We all used the big kitchen
with the range whose lid she lifted one day
when Stanley Gain (about my age,

but a boy, unfortunately)
came in dangling from a long stick something
murkily white with loops at each end:

'What's this, Mum?' 'I don't know; give it here' –
into the sizzling coals. He smirked and left.
She clanked the lid, and honoured me

with a complicit glance, as if
I were old enough to use things like that
or know what name she'd call them by.

Lost

She is prowling around the flat
all night, looking for the children.

Her granddaughter comes and tells her
they are safely tucked up in bed.

'No, not your children,' she says: 'Mine.
Where can they be? I can't find them.'

By daylight she finds us often:
two grown women, in our sixties.

Only in her dreams are we lost,
as sometimes she was lost in ours.

But what if we had found her then,
when we were still her little girls –

woken up in the night and found
a ninety-year-old great-granny

crying out in our mother's voice,
and no mother to comfort us?

Fleur Adcock's new collection, *Dragon Talk*
(her first since *Poems 1960 – 2000*) is to be
published by Bloodaxe in May 2010.

The Disappearing Kid

Geoff Nicholson

He blames his mother. Why not? Anyone would. Everybody does. She was the one who tried to make a man of him. And sure, his father played a part, did things to his mother that made her do things to her son, but dad wasn't around much, and then he wasn't there at all. He hadn't so much disappeared as slunk off. He could have been found, tracked down, made to pay, but what would have been the point? The abandonment only confirmed what she already knew, that she'd got involved with a characterless, weak, useless man. She was better off without him: his absence was a blessing.

She decided the son wouldn't be like the father. She didn't have specific ambitions for him, none of the familiar, self-serving maternal hopes for cleverness, money, prowess, charm; though in fact he would acquire all those things. She just didn't want him to be a weakling like his dad. That was her special project, her only one, to turn her boy into a little tough guy.

It went pretty well. The boy didn't resist. He learned that complaining did him no good. He learned not to be soft. He learned that if he got into trouble he had to get himself out. He liked the karate classes, the playground fights, the bullying, inflicting pain on others, denying it in himself. The little boy in him faded away. Was it tough love? Well, it was certainly tough.

His mother wasn't a bad woman; he decided long after the event. She had a lot of pain that she needed to medicate, but she took care of herself and him. And gradually her man-making project became more refined. Later when he tried to work out exactly how old he'd been when it first happened, he couldn't. There seemed to be no first time. It seemed to have been going on forever, always a part of his life, so it must have started when he was what? Six years old? Eight? Was that possible?

They were in the car. Mother and son travelling fast, no seat belts, no conversation. They'd been on an errand, picking up a load of towels that had fallen off the back of a lorry, but that had never been the real purpose of the trip. They were in a part of the city they'd been to before, though not often; commercial, light-industrial, some way from home, and suddenly she pulled the car over and said, "All right, time to get out."

"What?"

He wondered what he'd done wrong. His mother was an angry and moody woman. Anything could cause her to get mean and wild. It could be something somebody said to her, something she saw on TV, but more often than not, it was all his fault. But this time, oddly, she didn't sound angry. That was even more scary.

"We're going to make a man of you," she said. "So you don't end up like your father. Get out. I'll see you when you've found your way home."

She made it sound natural, the sort of thing all mothers and sons did, a game, something that could be fun, though since he was the only one playing it, he couldn't be sure about that.

"All right," he said, because no other reply was possible, and he got out.

He was still hoping, well, fantasizing more than hoping, because he knew how unlikely it was, that she'd smile and say forget it, it was all just a joke, a test, that she

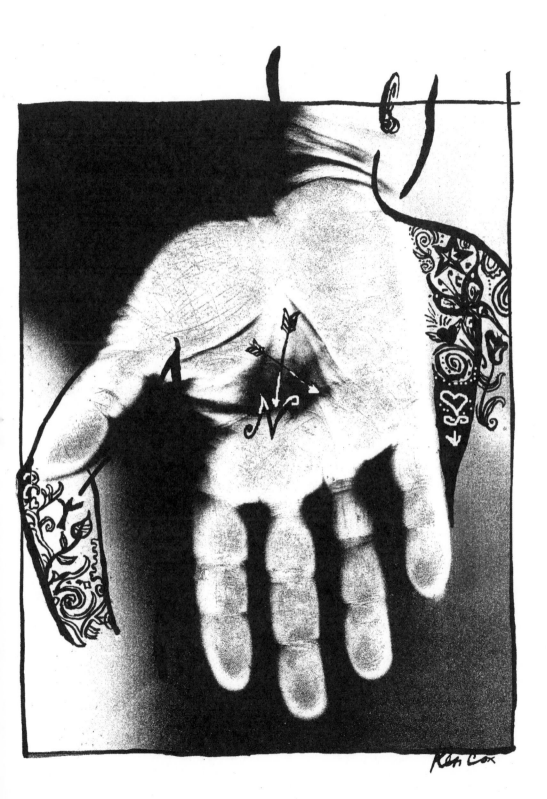

was trying to scare him, toughen him up, make sure he wasn't a cry baby. But he stood in the street and watched as his mother leaned over and yanked the door shut and drove away. She didn't wave goodbye.

He remained on the pavement, alone, lost, dry-eyed and he knew in some sense that he'd always be that way. He'd find his way home, all right. Of course he would. He knew his address, had a little money in his pocket and a tongue his head, he could ask people the way, he could get on a bus. He'd be OK.

And he was. He got home soon enough, without incident that time, and without much fear, and he supposed his mother was pleased to see him, though she didn't show it. And she must have been satisfied in some way because she did it again a week later, and again and again, regularly, all the time, dropping him off in ever more distant and dubious parts of the city.

He bought a map, small enough to be hidden in his back pocket. He hid it from her because he thought she might consider it cheating, not that he saw anything wrong with cheating. And so he always found his way back, and his mother was always there waiting, expectant, though she never seemed exactly glad to see him.

She succeeded in her way. She turned him into something he'd never been, and yes it bleached out any trace of weakness, any trace of his father. He knew he would never truly be lost, but also that he would never really be home. And eventually he never got lost at all. It became an impossibility. Wherever he was in the city, he belonged there. And even if he couldn't have precisely told you the name of the street or the district, it was only a matter of taking certain bearings, tuning into the geography, the slopes and flats of the city, noting the direction of the light, the angles of the skyline, and then he knew where he was: home.

Increasingly he saw no reason to hurry back to his mother. He began to dawdle, to explore. He began to get into trouble, to make trouble for himself. That was natural, that was the idea. This wasn't an exercise in keeping a clean nose, in staying on the straight and narrow. It was about taking the long way home, getting into scrapes, digging himself into holes, then extracting himself, working out what to do, surviving, flourishing.

Trouble came in various forms. There was the obvious stuff, the stuff he couldn't help doing, vandalism, minor theft, shoplifting, a bit of light pick-pocketing. He learned a lot from this. He learned about the separation of cause and effect, the unstable and unpredictable nature of consequences. He'd go into a store and lift half a dozen CDs, or go into a hardware store and steal as many screwdrivers and rolls of duct tape as he could hide in his clothing, and despite the hidden cameras and the security guards he'd get away with that completely. Nobody would notice; nobody would care. Other times he'd take a single apple from a market stall and find himself chased halfway round the neighbourhood by the stallholder. This was useful information.

But in general, if you saw this kid walking down the street, you wouldn't immediately think he was up to no good. He had a serious and purposeful air. There was the occasional concerned citizen who was interested to know if he was lost, where his parents were, why he wasn't at school, but he usually ignored them. If they got too interested he had a variety of answers of rising degrees of ferocity and obscenity, depending on just how firmly he wanted to make them mind their own fucking business.

And of course there was something you might call sex; men who invited him to get into cars with them, men who said they had something to show him, something to give him, something he'd be interested in. It always turned out to be a cock. It didn't happen often. Maybe he wasn't cute enough. Maybe he didn't look seducible. Maybe he just looked too much like trouble. And there was one guy who stopped his car and said his mother had sent him to take him home, but that was the one thing that couldn't be true.

But adults were far less of a problem than kids his own age. A boy on his own, even a tough little kid, away from home, not from the neighbourhood, well, that was an affront that couldn't go unchallenged. If they saw him looking at his map that got them really worked up. He had to be confronted. He had to be taught that he was in the wrong place. He was yelled at, tripped up, shouldered off the sidewalk, told to hand over his money. They always regretted it.

It wasn't that he always won the fights. He wasn't a superhero, and usually the kids were bigger than him and often they were in a group, but he always made them wish they'd never started it. They had no idea what they'd unleashed. There was something scary about the way he fought back; dirty, desperate, reckless.

Still, he knew his limits. He got good at knowing when to walk away. That always created a stir. He didn't feel humiliated by it, and it always got the other kids really angry. They'd call him a coward, a girl, a sissy, they'd throw things at him. But usually they'd let him go on his way. Usually they recognized that a kid who had the balls to turn his back and walk might be special in ways they didn't understand. But sometimes they were too stupid to recognize that, and then he had to run for his life.

He wasn't a bad runner, but there were limits here too. He reached that limit one afternoon round about his thirteenth birthday. It happened on a bleak winter day, backlit by a furred grey sky, with the threat of snow in the air, and there on a corner lounging by a traffic light, were two kids who looked like fair game. They were foreign, very foreign, skins purple black. They looked out of place, and they'd have looked out of place anywhere in this city. They were gawky, elongated, their limbs seemed to have too many segments, too many joints. And they were so improbably tall. They were slouching, leaning on a railing, heads hanging, and even so they towered above him: yet still, they did look like geeks, and he couldn't walk past a pair of geeks without doing or saying something.

Afterwards he wondered if maybe they were young marathon runners in exile, but at the time that didn't seem very likely: they were smoking handrolled cigarettes. They might have been joints for all he knew, certainly they were being handled furtively, and the boys looked around once in a while to see if the coast was clear before inhaling deeply.

And as he walked by them he said, couldn't help saying, "Hey boys, don't smoke. It'll stunt your growth." And really, how bad a thing was that to say? It was a joke, not even a real insult; but they reacted as if he'd accused their mothers of doing things with monkeys. In fact he wondered if they hadn't really heard what he said, or didn't understand the language, and certainly they didn't say anything back, but he got the clear message that they were going to avenge themselves on him.

The two boys straightened up, seemed to unfold. They looked regal and infinitely dangerous and he knew they had plans to extract the living daylights from him. He began to run, faster, more determinedly than he'd ever run before. Why was he so scared? Was it because they were black? Maybe. Certainly it was because they were so alien. He didn't know what rules they'd play by if, when, they caught him.

They ran beautifully. They had style and rhythm. He felt himself to be a flurry of contradictory impulses; arms, legs and lungs working at odds, whereas these guys were all fluid motion, effortless, spindly legs scarcely touching the ground. He got the feeling they were toying with him, not even trying to catch him. They could have pounced whenever they wanted to, but they didn't want to, not yet, they were just exhausting him for the fun of it. He kept going as long as he could. It was a brave effort but he knew he was running out of juice.

One way or another, things were coming to a conclusion: the chase was coming to an end. He needed to get off the street, find some protected space, a shop, a café, maybe a bank, somewhere they wouldn't follow and where they surely wouldn't attack him even if they did. His eyes were watering with the exertion, and the street around him was looking blurred and grubby, but if there were going to be salvation it would have to be here. There was a row of small shops with signs he could only barely make out; an off licence, a head shop, a place that sold old-fashioned stationery. He didn't like the look of any of them, and careened past, and then he'd run out of all options but one. There was only one door, one shop left. He had to go for it whatever it was.

He dashed up to the glass front door, didn't look inside, opened it just enough to slide through, then slammed it behind him and leaned up against it, gulping for air. His mind was empty and he didn't know what he'd walked into. He blinked about him, trying to work it out. It was very bright and quiet in here, and his first thought was he'd come into a dentist's. There was even a noise from the back of the store that sounded like a dentist's drill, and there was definitely somebody laid out back there, a woman who seemed to be suffering.

However, the person who was doing the drilling didn't look remotely like a dentist. She had long black hair and tight black jeans and bare arms, one of which had a sleeve of tattoos. She stopped what she was doing and said, "What's the matter kid? Hell hound on your trail?" and that didn't sound like the kind of thing a dentist would say. Then he noticed there were pictures all over the walls, bright colors and clear lines; skulls, dancing girls, flames, hotrods, devils. He was smart enough to know he was in a tattooist's studio.

"No," he said seriously, between breaths, "not hell hounds," and he looked out through the window and saw the two tall, thin black kids across the street, waiting, pacing languidly up and down, displaying a chilly impatience.

"Are those two giving you grief?" the tattooist said.

He wasn't a squealer. He didn't need to be. It was obvious. The tattooist said to the woman on the table, "Hold on babe," rummaged in a metal cabinet and pro-duced – he could hardly believe it – a crossbow. It looked modern rather than ancient; a frame of brushed metal, a telescopic sight, a rifle stock. It was a terrifying thing even to look at. The tattooist went to the door, opened it, cocked the crossbow, inserted the stubby arrow and fired across the street. She didn't seem to be aiming at anything in particular and yet the arrow bisected the space between the two boys perfectly, lodging neatly in a telephone pole. The boys yelled something in an unrec-ognizable tongue and ran off, much faster and harder than they'd run before. The tat-tooist shouted after them, "Piss off you little racists."

Back in the tattoo studio, the kid was shocked and impressed, and just a little con-fused. He'd confessed to needing help. A woman had come to his aid. Why did that feel so good? He laughed boyishly, unselfconsciously. He didn't laugh like that very often.

146

"You can call me Rose," said the tattooist.

"I'm Ray," the boy said.

"Are you? Make yourself at home, Ray. And come over here and watch an artist at work."

She returned to her customer, her tattooing. The woman on the table was lying prone with her arms bare and raised high above her head. There was a length of yellow silk draped across her breasts, though she didn't seem much concerned with modesty. She had other things on her mind, or perhaps nothing at all. Her eyes were open but they weren't looking at anything in particular. She was moaning quietly to herself but Ray didn't know if it was pain or something else.

"Is she all right?" he asked.

"Yeah. She's fine," said Rose. "She's full of endorphins."

"What's that?"

"Chemicals. When you're in pain the body releases these things called endorphins. They make the pain feel good after a while. Got that?"

"I think so," Ray said, though he wasn't sure he did.

"This young lady is in the middle of an endorphin rush," said Rose. "That's because I'm tattooing her armpits. That hurts like fuck, doesn't it babe?"

"Oh yes," said the woman on the table. "Oh yes."

Ray peered into her left armpit, then the right. In the left the tattoo was already completed, while the right was still a work in progress. When finished, the tattoos would be identical representations of whirlpools, swirls of blue, white and purple, something gothic and Japanese about them. They weren't the only tattoos the woman had. There were stars, swallows, poppies, butterflies, jungle creepers twining their way up her arms. There was a winged heart on her chest, peeping out above the yellow silk, but Ray found himself transfixed by the armpit tattoos, the sheer weirdness of them. Why would she choose so much pain for a tattoo that so few would ever see? He didn't expect to be given an explanation.

Rose worked hard at her tattooing, with a scary intensity. She didn't say much and the other woman said even less, so Ray kept his mouth shut too. It went on for a long time, and although Ray could see it was a delicate, painstaking process, after a while the work itself wasn't so fascinating a spectacle. The woman's face however, that was something else, something special. Within a frame of thick, tangled blonde hair her features were mobile and alive, alternating between certain pain and uncertain pleasure: lip-biting, tears in the eyes, a trembling mouth that was close to laughter but not close enough,

Ray stayed till the very end of the process, until Rose was finished and the woman was thoroughly inked and wiped down, then sitting up, holding a mirror to her armpits to see the final effect. She was more pleased with them than Ray would have thought possible. He actually thought the whirlpools looked a bit crappy, that maybe Rose wasn't the greatest tattooist, but perhaps that didn't matter. He was far more impressed by how pleased the woman was, how happy Rose was with her own handiwork.

"Can I have one?" Ray asked.

"What? A tattoo?" said Rose.

"Yeah."

"No you can't."

"Why not?"

"Because I don't want to go to jail. Tattooing kids is still illegal in this town."

"Oh go on," said the newly tattooed customer.

"Are you trying to get me into trouble?"

"Always," she said, "but you could just do something really small, something nobody would ever see."

"Like in my armpit," said Ray.

"Oh yeah right."

"Go on Rose," said the woman.

It seemed that Rose had a hard time saying no to her.

"OK kid, gimme your hand."

Eagerly Ray extended his right hand, balled into a fist. He was already picturing a Viking or a fireball emblazoned across his knuckles, but Rose grabbed the hand, rolled it over and opened it up, and as quickly and as perfunctorily as possible made a few small blue-black ink marks on Ray's palm: a circle, a pair of crossed arrows, one of them marked with an N for north, forming a rudimentary compass rose.

"If anybody asks, you did it to yourself," she said.

"OK," said Ray.

But nobody did ask him. He went home, went back to his mother, went on with his life of losing and finding, and nobody ever said to him, "What's that on the palm of your hand?" No doubt there were other boys with lives that included the inspecting of hands, for cleanliness, honesty, maybe even punishment, but Ray had none of that. He kept his hand to himself. He only ever looked at it, stared at it, when he was alone, when nobody else was looking. Still, that was often enough to realize, all too soon, after just a couple of weeks, that the tattooed marks were fading.

At first he felt disappointed, then cheated. Rose must have known this would happen, that the marks would disappear. That's what happens to tattoos on the palm of a hand, they just fade away. She'd tricked him, treated him like a child. But then he started to feel differently. Maybe Rose had been pretty smart. She'd done the job, done what Ray had asked of her, done what her girlfriend had urged her to do and yet she'd also allowed for a reversal, for second thoughts, and made sure that she didn't end up in jail for tattooing a kid.

Ray needed to talk to her about this, and so he went off, threading his way into the city to find her again, attempting to retrace the route that had taken him there that day. Of course he'd had other things on his mind at the time; panic, fear, the exhilarating, painful need to escape. Even so he was surprised to find how alien the district looked, how hard it was to find a landmark that told him he was anywhere near the right place. He thought, he was pretty sure, that he'd found the spot where he first encountered his pursuers, and he had some notion of the direction he'd gone, a general idea of the area he'd run through. But perhaps he was mistaken. Perhaps he hadn't run this way at all. Certainly it all looked unfamiliar, and he definitely couldn't find the off licence and the head shop, which meant that he couldn't possibly find Rose's tattoo studio. He spent the whole afternoon covering the area, walking back and forth, pacing the grid, looking for clues, looking out also in case he might meet two tall, black kids who liked to run. But he found nothing. And in the end he knew there was nothing to be found. The day, the row of shops, Rose, the studio, had all disappeared just like his tattoo, just like his father.

Geoff Nicholson's books include *Bleeding London*, *Gravity's Volkswagen* and *The Lost Art of Walking*. 'The Disappearing Kid' is an extract from a work in regress, currently called *Skinned City*.

John Morgan studio designed this ad for the 200th issue of Ambit.

Ambit 200 Words Competition

Judging the *Ambit* 200 Words competition was a complicated task. Poetry, prose and prose-poetry were submitted and we found it hard to compare pieces written with obviously quite different intentions, one issue being the relative weighting of technical accomplishment and emotional heft. But fortunately the winners were obvious. First Prize clearly belonged to 'Yesenia Gets on the 26 Bus', which crackled from the first line, its vitality and warmth only deepening as the story develops to its painful conclusion. One wonders if the writer is also a poet: the two dancing, punchy anapaestic feet in the penultimate line are, in context, cruelly ironic, while the final use of iambic pentameter ends this story of cultural and other collisions on a sub-liminally Shakespearean note. We gave second prize to 'Nelly', for the extremely enjoyable linguistic vigour, dexterity and humour with which it delineates both par-ties to its May – December non-romance. When it came to third place, we were both struck by 'Persephone': the opening imagery stiflingly evokes more recent horror stories – the courage and endurance of Elizabeth Fritzl came to mind – while in his or her perceptive treatment of the pomegranate seeds, the writer achieves an origi-nal slant on a very old story. Having received permission to split third prize, we also happily included 'Acorns' in the winner's circle, having both admired its quiet sym-bolism and poetic grace. We were also especially impressed by the technical accom-plishment and film noir atmosphere of 'The Leak'; the surreal narrative strategies of 'Theatre'; and the sustained yet subtle creepiness of 'Ears'.

Reading all this new work all in one go was also a good way to test the psyche of the writers in the country: what were all these talented scribes thinking about in early 2010? What would be the common themes? Well, we got people nailing their pubic hair to the walls of their house, Glaswegian male feminists bemoaning the return of stiletto heels, a duck trained to be a ruthless killer, stories formatted as GP referral let-ters, stories laid out in little boxes, stories made up from quirkily translated instruc-tion manuals, and a poem based on Lars Von Trier's Dogme film making manifesto. There were sex scenes – some bestial thrusting from one person in fact – but oddly enough, very little swearing; maybe with a 200 word limit a swear word is wasteful. In the stories there were circuses, magicians, myths, comedy. In the poetry, Russian gulags, fish and insects, origami birds and suicide pacts. The influences were various – the ghosts of Eggers, Brautingham, Keret, Rhodes, could be detected in the styles of many while John Clare, Tennyson, Billy Collins and Michael Donaghy, Emily Dick-inson, Dylan Thomas and Jenny Joseph made guest appearances in the poems, the latter three in prose sonnets, perhaps a new form the competition birthed. But did the work say anything about now? No, not really. There was nothing about evil bankers, nothing about hung parliaments, a bit about the environment, but not much, and nothing about the BNP. It was the usual sex and death really, business as ever from us writers. Planting and food were abundant (do many writers have allotments?) and two out of our final six had something to do with eggs. The entire selection was more rural than urban. Three of our top seven directly confront the issue of violence against women. Two empower the woman by giving her a voice, while the winning story is imbued with the compassion of a witness to the aftermath of Yesinia's ordeal. We dare to hope that the prevalence of this theme in the more strongly-written entries is part of a general move toward exposing this cultural cancer.

We had many more excellent entries than we could give prizes to. There were a few which had the makings of greatness but needed that bit more tweaking, and some that had been tweaked too far and needed to be left somewhere on their own to relax.

We hope that our choice of winners make a difference to the writers selected and that this competition will bring thrilling and innovative writing to new audiences.

First Prize

Yesenia Gets on the 26 Bus *Jennifer Olds*

At the beginning of the semester, Yesenia rocked a tight ponytail, shoulders back, new books loading her backpack as she jumped from the 26 bus and bopped across the lot to class. She read Emerson first, wrote 'Gang-banging Half-Gods of the Barrio', scored highly on the pre-nursing exams, winked and said, 'Dr Honey-babe, I wanna see some real gods arrive, if you know what I mean.'

Last week, she swayed to her iPod, said her new man – a strong man, a neighbourhood giant – had a lightning bolt tattooed on his shaved head.

Today she let her hair swing from a center part to hide her face. She wore her hood up, not down, did not say, 'So Walden is a false utopia but that don't mean it was dystopic' or 'What is it with Thoreau and women cuz the man had no babes.'

From the doorframe of the classroom, I watch her go.

When she moves through the lot to the 26 bus, her steps are uncertain. One arm cradles her ribs, raw as a baby.

She looks like her half-god has hit her.

She looks like he has thrown her down the stairs.

Jennifer Olds is a professor in Southern California. Her work was shortlisted for the 2009 Bridport Prize in both poetry and fiction categories, and her poetry collections include *Rodeo and the Mimosa Tree* (Event Horizon), *The Half-Acre Ranch* (First Edition, UK), and *An Extra Half-Acre* (First Edition, UK). Her novel, *Good-Night, Henry*, was published by Penguin/NAL in 2005. She has just completed her next poetry collection, *Polo for Losers*, and is finalizing a book of linked short stories, *Heifer World*. Jennifer enjoys roping steers, playing polo, and shooting pool, but not simultaneously. Her husband is renowned for his patience.

Second Prize

Nelly *Tony Dash*

Nelly wore a frock of crows
and played her carrion music,
saving the blue notes for me.
Nelly wore a cloak of lies,
while her Walls-of-Jericho-Girdle
slipped down, to reveal deep mysteries.

Nelly wanted hot doings.
I used to want hot doings.
But she called me unprepossessive,
said I was a bit crabbed and grim.
Enrol at a Lazaretto,
she said, your body, is nothing

but a shrivelled skin-bag,
it has no deep mysteries,
only your stiff spine and wattled throat,
only creaky tibias and shrunk genitals,
only stumbling feet and disappearing teeth.
In short, you are rebarbative.

I might have a small island I told her,
I might have engravers, dressmakers.
I might have pedestals and votive offerings,
I could do marvelling and swooning
whatever it might take to please her.
Old rat sweat! Nelly cried,

show me the beauty of unlaid eggs.
I couldn't – didn't know how to.
But *did* know how to run up and down
our sofa, knocking my head against
the wood panel in a ritual display
of my gift for tragic irony.

All this time choking on the wrong idol,
neglecting my ambition to survive
a parade of withered grandchildren.

Tony Dash is a poet, fiction writer, artist and publisher who lives in Liverpool.

Third Prize: Joint Winners

Persephone *Rosie Jackson*

I can't tell you the terror of being down there.
All those miles of earth on top of me – the stench, the dark –
and him on top, paddling my thin body like a piece of dough.
The worse thing is the trick of memory:
not knowing if you've imagined the shape of a mother
the flimsiness of a dandelion seed
the joy of a feather.
No days there, only nights back to back,
crawling through the underworld like a badger.
All I had were the six pomegranate seeds
I hid in my pocket that afternoon of my capture,
little garnet beads, fingering them over and over.
I ate one at each time of bleeding:
they were my salvation, my hope, my calendar,
knowing once they were gone
I would find the rope to climb back to the sun.
If you'd been there you would live it as I do,
this renewed miracle of sun on skin.
You would spend your heart and eat,
eat well the shoots and herbs
and leaves and oranges, save only this:
one pomegranate fruit to take with you as a bait
to recapture the sun
when you go down again
into that long labyrinth of winter.

Rosie Jackson writes novels, stories, poems and creative non-fiction. Her books
include *Fantasy: The Literature of Subversion*, *Frieda Lawrence*, *Mothers Who Leave*
and *The Eye of the Buddha*. Her story `What the Water Gave Me' won the 2006 Writers
Inc. Writers of the Year award.

www.rosiejackson.org.uk

Acorns *Maj Abrahamsson*

He walked off one day. His footprints were deep and muddy, and I put seeds into them. I planted trees in his mud and they grew higher every year. He walked off one day through the clouds of our little world. He walked in his best outfit, out of the frame. The chipped gold-painted frame embedded with acorns. They were there as decoration, those acorns, and they reminded me of myself.

Our house was very small for one person, but just right for two. Nowhere to escape so we always ended up in each other's arms. We had hens. Heavy frail-winged hens and the yolks of their eggs were as yellow as chanterelles, as sun on newly cut wood, as psalms. But I bore no eggs. And one day, he walked off.

I hoped for rain. Dense rain like nails so he would have to turn back. I hoped for snow, but it was May, and I hoped in vain. I prayed. His clothes sprawled over our floor were my altar. Weeks passed before I felt it stir. The flimsy residue he had left behind. The grasping in my belly where no one had lived before. And the wetness of moss after rain.

Maj Abrahamsson grew up in the countryside in Sweden and used to write all over her wallpaper. Now she lives in london where she studies illustration and writes in the hundreds of notebooks her stationery-fetish has provided. Her favourite things are painting, getting lost, eating cake and drinking too much coffee.

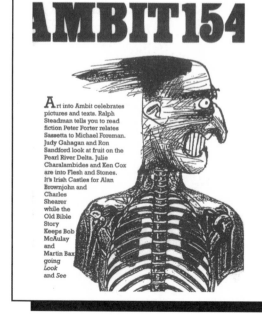

Reviews

We are opening *Ambit 200*'s review section with two reviews of Herbert Lomas's *A Casual Knack of Living: Collected Poems* (Arc Publications £13.49). Bertie was one of *Ambit*'s regular reviewers for thirty years and we are thus rewarding him with extra coverage.

Helena Nelson on
A Casual Knack of Living

This a beautiful book. I have the advantage of possessing the hardback edition, now out of print. However, the paperback also sports that gorgeous painting of the sea front at Aldeburgh, the casual fellow with his bike, the sun on the water. It is a big book too: it runs to 400 pages of poems drawn from nine previously published collections, with a final section of nearly fifty uncollected pieces. So what you've got here is a lifetime of poetry. It is Herbert Lomas's whole self.

Or that's what it felt like to me, dipping in, sifting the poems with the same pleasure you get from handling pebbles on Norfolk beaches. There's a disarming honesty in this poet who opens up his life stanza by stanza. Sometimes you empathise; sometimes you don't, but all of it is plain and true. And he never ever makes you feel stupid or gets caught up in his own cleverness. He is wry and funny and intelligent and insightful and heart-breaking – all of these things and more. 'First Kisses', for example:

*[...] late at night, comforting
someone in tears. Perhaps it's because
she's so hot with suffering, or hasn't
used her kissing mouth for almost years.
But probably not: she just has a talent
and like so many talents,
it's been buried.*

Or 'Distance', with the white space opening out between the lines like sorrow – (this is the complete poem):

*A sad bald man is taking a solitary walk by the
sea.*

Daffodils push through the withered bracken.

*A bird keeps hammering three notes on a tiny
anvil.*

Even at this late hour a child's out with his kite.

*I've fallen in love with someone no one can live
with.*

Blurb writers on the back of books by 'new' 'innovative' young poets wax lyrical about 'risk-taking'. Look at the risks here and marvel at this elderly poet's method, his music, his mayhem. He is never boring. He is modestly magnificent. And you can live with him at your bedside for years.

Tim Liardet on
A Casual Knack of Living

Bertie Lomas's handsome *Collected Poems* is a formidable volume. There is something strangely moving as it travels serenely from collection to collection, poem to poem. In the surprisingly short 'A Word', by way of introduction, Lomas quotes Tennyson approvingly: 'men may rise on stepping stones / of their dead selves'. He doesn't share with us, however, whether he succumbed to the potential madness of attempting to bring poems written years before up to date. Was there tinkering? If he was embarrassed by his cockier, younger selves – to paraphrase Peter Porter – he doesn't act the prig to them. Either way, the harvest, or at least the majority of the harvest, is in, and the book weighs heavy in the hand.

It moves in a sort of cyclical motion, starting out with the poem 'Chimpanzees are Blameless Creatures', in 1969, and ending, forty-one years later – though there's a sense that only five minutes might have elapsed – with 'The Skin is Greater than the Banana'. Tonally and existentially, these two expansive titles and the poems that accrete to them seem to have much in common with one another. To put it another way, the book starts out with one of our principal evolutionary relatives and ends with what they are fed.

What's most impressive about Lomas's oeuvre, seen in one grasp, is the alacrity with which his former selves animate themselves on the page. The Tennysonian stepping stones are well demarcated. Here is the young post-Georgian in 1969, subverting the love-lyric, from 'True Love':

155

In the dark scented air
of coal dust and cat piss
two infant lovers stare
and shyly kiss.

Here is his rather less gauche successor,
some twelve years later, showing younger and
older poets alike what it takes to obviate the
potential euphonic death-rattle of a villanelle,
with some dynamism, in 'Retreat to the
Sheets', from *Public Footpath:*

My cat approves of these long slow afternoons –
A day in bed, a headache, grey outside.
These days in bed are always opportune.

Despair's close by – and who can be immune?
You need new time, to brew unoccupied,
Which makes my cat enjoy these afternoons.

And here he is, some sixty or more years later,
from the unpublished sequence 'Nightlights',
seven years into the new Millennium, still
retaining all the old mischief; final proof the
essential twinkle of his first collection in 1969
is still twinkling:

A turd
    is neither obscene nor absurd.
A turd
    is a divine invention,
    like a bird

These extracts of a man's evolution first come
together as scraps of footage in the mind.
No one would expect them to cohere into an
ordered poetic consciousness. Thought and
emotional intelligence rarely develop in a
straight line. The extracts sharpen and blur,
move on. They offer up, instead, the fragments
of which the consciousness is comprised – the
bits and pieces, the consistencies and contra-
dictions which glue together to make Lomas
the man and poet he is. Once I'd closed the book
I was left with the likeness of an Arcimboldo
portrait – a man carrying in his countenance all
he had ever been, ever would be. This is a haunting book. Its principle strengths are diversity,
movement, the intensity of world-wonder. Rein-
forcing Larkin's dictum that we have no choice
about the poetry we write, however much
Lomas's poetry changes, it somehow remains
the same; however much it remains the same,
it changes.

In the Wake of the Day
John Ash
Carcanet £9.95

Take a trip with John Ash. That's a curious way
to begin a review but it's how I feel when I
start to read one of his poems. They seem to
invite me on board and then carry me along
with their seemingly casual way of dealing
with people and events. Here are some lines
that might be said to be typical:

The boys at the next table were getting
                                            emotional.
One stood up and made as if to leave, but was
Persuaded to stay. Another wept copiously.
The handsomest youth was the one who
                                            remained calm,
And reasoned with the rest. But what could
                                            have inspired
Such a collective fit of passion? Intrigued,
I introduced myself. At once, they insisted
That I join them, and summoned the musicians.
Then the questions began. Where was I from?
What was I doing in Ankara? Where did I live?
Where was I going? How far, how long, and
                                            why?

The poem develops like a travelogue, though
with the poet and his new-found friends at its
centre and with vivid descriptions of places
visited. And the 'seemingly casual' approach
that I mentioned earlier is, of course, a well-
crafted way of constructing a poem so that it
appears to be relaxed and easy to read. The
technique is unobtrusive, which is as it should
be. It's what the poems say that counts.

A couple of the poems favourably mention
the fine American poet, Kenneth Koch, and it's
not hard to know why. Ash, without imitating,
has the same good-humoured tone evident in
his poems. And the reader always knows what
he's talking about. There's a lot to be found in
Ash's poems and he's not afraid to refer to his-
torical events, other writers, classical composers, and much more. He's not a populist,
despite writing directly and openly. But he can
be sly and I like his lines which say:

Poetry is always difficult
Like a maladjusted child,
But perhaps it should only be
Difficult for the poet, not the reader.

Jim Burns

Through the Square Window
Sinead Morrissey
Carcanet £9.95

This is a nicely varied collection, though I have to admit to preferring some poems to others. I suppose my liking for fairly straightforward writing which deals with everyday life and its ups and downs inclines me to favour certain items. There's a fine poem called 'Fairground Music' which tells the story of a girl having a miscarriage. It starts quietly enough:

The fair had come. It must have been Whitsun.
They'd camp every year at the end of our yard –
you could hear the screams and the grinding of
the rides
and a noise like whiz-bangs from the house.

But it soon moves on to the girl calling to ask if she can use the privy. She is outside for some time and then leaves, 'grey as a newspaper'. The narrator goes out to check: 'Inside, blood was everywhere: on the floor, on the walls. / You could tell where Esther had walked / by a set of white shadows.' It builds up to a bleak ending that leaves the reader as shocked as the narrator.

The everyday isn't always that harsh, of course, and there are good poems about family life and about childhood. 'The Hanging Hare' effectively presents itself on the page in a shaped pattern and has a strong visual element in the writing, and 'Missing Winter' evokes time and place:

Though the four 'clock dark
is massed, obliterating –
winter comes careening
in storms over the Shore Park,
its hair undone and the back door banging.

At this point I ought to explain why I prefer these poems to others which are admittedly well-written but, for me, less interesting. Poems such as 'Vanity Fair' and 'The Innocents' don't add much to what I already know about the stories they're based on. And a poem like 'York' has that feeling of something produced when there wasn't anything else to write about. I'm possibly being unfair when I say this and all poets probably write a certain amount just to keep the ball rolling, so to speak. *Jim Burns*

Everyday Angels
Maria Jastrzebska
Waterloo Press £10

Good poems can be made from quite mundane subjects. Maria Jastrzebska has one about paraffin stoves:

Fat black, they almost
had faces. I'd watch the orange
shapes they cast gyrating
on the walls. I loved our old heaters,
the rough paraffin smell.

The poem goes on to tell how the family live with this kind of heating, the mother complaining all the time, but eventually switch to central heating: 'The house was warmer. / but a spark had gone.' I suppose it's a fairly typical kind of lament for the loss of old values and experiences, but it works well because of the easy rhythms and the clarity of the writing.

The clarity is evident in most of the poems in this book. They tell stories, often of life among Polish immigrants to Britain who sometimes meet with hostility ('Bloody foreigners. Go back where you came from.') They remember the old country and get together for warmth and friendship, though sometimes the meetings don't always result in relaxed relationships. A prose poem called 'Holy Night' has the narrator's mother quarrelling with her mother: 'It's all because of you, why did you make me come to this god-forsaken country, I hate this bloody place, why did you make us come.' You get a strong feeling from these lines of the uneasiness that can mark the lives of people who are not really at home in their adopted country.

I don't want to give the impression that all the poems in *Everyday Angels* are like this. There are decent pieces about opera, Shoreham Harbour, and one which lightly mocks a doctor's advice to ME sufferers to only do 75 per cent of what they normally do and then rest: 'Three quarters of the way / to an orgasm, and then, what?'

This is a friendly book that should appeal to those who like to think of poetry as a pleasure rather than a puzzle. *Jim Burns*

The Breakfast Room
Stewart Conn
Bloodaxe £8.95

Of Stewart Conn's first collection, *Stars in Twilight* (1968), the Third Programme (now Radio 3) said: 'The classical qualities of clear, rather grave cadences, straightforward though supple lineation, the timing of each verse beautifully varied according to sense…' (Was that awkward eulogy written by the late and kindly George MacBeth?)

The Breakfast Room shows how Conn has lost those 'grave cadences' – to his advantage. There is a lighter, wittier touch; poems by a writer on the top of his form.

The lightness is shown in 'Prizes':

Two writers agree that the prize doesn't matter: one has won it, the other hasn't.

★

*At my age, surely no one supposes
I give a toss who wins this prize*

*or that. Tell them, if the phone goes,
I'm outside – dead-heading the roses.*

The title poem tackles that trickiest of subjects, a painter's picture, here Bonnard's 'The Breakfast Room' – or is it? How about Marthe in her bathtub? It ends:

*[…]
hence my depictions of her as Venus emerging
the light casting a spell on her skin as it was
when I first met her. A vision of young love
preserved, my palette imbues her with the
blue-violet of memory. No need to choose
betweensmelling the scent and plucking the
flower –painting her has been like bottling a
rare spirit. Now, if you'll excuse me, I have
a bath to run.*

'Sleepless Night' is reminiscent of Larkin's 'Arundel Tomb', but almost certainly written without a backward glance. 'Carpe Diem' also echoes (Hardy?):

*And my heart misses a beat
    at love for you.
Knowing a time will come
    when you are
no longer there, nor I here
    to watch you*

*on a day of such simplicity
    Meantime let us*

*make sure we clasp each
    shared moment
in cupped hands, like water
    we dare not spill.*

'He stands among the indispensable poets of modern and contemporary Scotland', wrote Douglas Dunn in *The Dark Horse* (1995–). He could, perhaps, have dispensed with that 'Scotland'. *Barry Cole*

Looking out, Looking In: New and Selected Poems
E. A. Markham
Anvil £14.95

Receiving this collection jogged a memory: I had reviewed him before – *Letter from Ulster and The Hugo Poems* (1993) – and found, tipped in, my notes. But I cannot remember for whom they were written. The point is that some of them could apply to this new and sadly last collection: 'A Poet of the World' has '…Fear / of stretching out foot from Montserrat, / and falling into the sea. In France, in Germany, / in spray-white Sweden…' Not just a poet of the world, but a citizen of it – from Papua New Guinea (a travel book which ought to be reprinted) to London, Northern Ireland, Africa and, finally, Paris, where he died in 2008.

This is a fat and handsome collection from almost all of his (poetry) books except the very rare *Love Poems* (Lobby Press, 1978), and he is so varied a writer that only extensive quotations can ever hint at his remarkable talent – he seems to have been born a poet. The following is from 'Homage to an Old Master', about Louis XIV:

*Some boys said in those days you could
replace your own teeth with those of a poor
                                            man
caught in the street, or you could have teeth
                                            made
from a hard wood like greenheart, sewn into
your mouth and painted, so who's to know
                                    they weren't
your own except the wife when she kissed you;
for she would have to be careful of splinters.
And we pitied the mouth of the Queen of
                                        France.*

(The Old Master was a teacher). Or these lines, from 'Little Miracles':

It's a bad time, your book
Is no consolation. Past midnight
And your present partner has not
Been identified. It's raining
On the tramps in the street.
Past midnight, time for the medicine.
And when the book fails to satisfy
Gives praise to the mind's rebellion.
For the partner, there's still
A hundred and ninety-five countries
In the world. For you and the tramps
It will be morning. Soon.

His last poem? It's portentous, moving, and suggests, in all those countries, that he is calling into account a great part of his wandering life. I'm puzzled by the capital letters at the start of each line (it's a rarity), but no doubt he would tell me I was being obtuse.

Of the many other poems which attract is 'John Lewis' (2003), a 'Little Play with Interludes', a tour de force of social and personal comment, and probably the closest he gets to a synthesis of his many styles, moods and modes.

Peter Porter, in *Towards the End of a Century* (1989), wrote that Markham reasserts his place 'as a leading literary figure and poet'. Nothing has changed. He was (*b.* 1939) one of the finest poets of his generation.
Barry Cole

Picasso, I Want My Face Back
Grace Nichols
Bloodaxe £7.95

In his 1937 painting *Weeping Woman*, Picasso married hard lines with soft, a gaudy palette with greyscale, mimesis with anatomical improbabilities. And somehow he created a coherent, gestalt entity. Grace Nichols, in her latest collection of a career well into its third decade, attempts a similar trick without quite pulling it off.

Twenty interlocking sections make up the long opening poem, each afforded its own stylistic treatment. It's written in the voice of Dora Maar, the 'weeping woman' herself, and one of Picasso's most famous muses. In her preface, Nichols explains that she was compelled to 'give that face a voice'. 'Picasso, I Want My Face Back' is the result. It begins:

They say that instead of a brush
he used a knife on me –
a savage geometry.
But I say, look again,
this is the closest
anyone has got to the pain.

Maar, who suffered a breakdown when her ten-year relationship with Picasso ended, begins jostling, testing the artist and his visually violent treatment of her. Nichols twists her through various feelings: anger and melancholy, jealousy and spite. Ultimately Maar transcends the painting, no longer 'imprisoned in that cocoon'; she 'bloom[s] everywhere', free to grow in her own space, on her own terms.

Although the tale is celebratory, the telling, sadly, is not. Nabokov argued that great literature isn't registered in the heart or the brain, but in the spine, the place where the 'telltale tingle' strikes. Nichols' work appeals to the heart, unquestionably, and the brain is given enough fuel to fire. But despite the frequent garlicy moments, that tingle never quite arrives.

Green knows me –
Not the green of new shoots
but the ghastly green of gangrene.

Nichols draws a distinction between two tired opposites – we all know the colour of new shoots and gangrene. Poetry's role isn't one of consolation; surely it ought to surprise and move us.

That said, there is much to savour in these poems, the rhythms of which flourish when spoken aloud. Each of the four sections – 'Picasso, I Want My Face Back', 'Framing the Landscape', 'Eclipse' and 'Laughing Woman' – ends on a soaring note; if only it sounded more often. A poem comprised of six lovely, trickling lines, closes the collection, and is demonstrative of the dazzling pitch Nichols attains once in a while. It's entitled 'Even in the Midst':

Even in the midst of dwelling
on the thorns of history
tickle her with the memory
of one silly story –
then sit back and reap
the peals of an abundant harvest

Gary Cansell

Gina Wisker

Candles in the Dark

We're not sure how to grow old, we baby boomers we
first generation into university types whether
high achievers or just surprised at mortgages and kids and anniversaries the
deaths of parents, and partners, we
are bemused, sold perhaps on progress
and consumer goods, or uneasily cherishing instead
their balancing against some ethical vision, some
ecological commitment, some hippy remnant maybe
of that other period, the war shocked, celebratory, music,
substance, dream, alternative – that poetic contradiction, that
east west embrace and not hostility of now.
Amid the rumbling desert tanks, the border crossing explosions and
the pyres of tall buildings, how do we age?
Sold out or sold up, broken or unbroken,
power down or power up, how
embrace the promise of long days in the sunshine in our gardens that
drift into the insubstantiality of dream turned dementia;
develop a time and taste for words, music, travel or
lose each and all of these to surprise, invasive lumps and overwhelming
inarticulacy, he falling worth of investments and the
refusal of dependents to become
independent?
Negative equities and energies bombard us.
A nasty sense of being tricked. No nirvana these
last fumbling years of, if you're lucky,
at least not perpetual nagging pain and debt .
If glimpsed still there at rock concerts, for how long will we
be seeking shelter? out there, singing 'forever young' and holding
hopeful candles in the dark
and wind?

Gina Wisker lives in Cambridge and works in Brighton. She is co-editor of (now
online) poetry magazine *Spokes* and online dark fantasy/horror journal *Dissections*.
Her poetry and short fiction have been published in (among others) *Femspec*,
Running On Empty and *Women's Words*, and she has two books of poetry from
Calypso Press – *Pearls* (with Deena Warner) and *Fixtures and Fissures*.

The Lavenham Press Limited

printers of this magazine

A horse hair factory may sound like an unlikely building for a printing press, but in the fifties it caught the eye of Terence Dalton, father of the present director of the Lavenham Press. Abandoning the turbulent world of London printing, he persuaded two of his staff to join him, took some printing machinery to a village north of Sudbury, and founded the Lavenham Press.

Now, some sixty years later, the press looks somewhat different. Two vast Heidelberg five-colour printing machines dominate the factory, producing fifteen thousand sheets an hour. With digital printers available for short-run work, the range and quality of printing that Lavenham now produces is impressive.

The press serves a wide range of customers, printing everything from scientific journals, such as the prestigious Journal of the Royal College of Physicians, to books printed for private customers.

No wonder every Ambit since issue six in 1960 has been printed by the Lavenham Press. To celebrate this long association, the press is proud to sponsor the next thirty-six pages of this voluptuous edition.

The Lavenham Press Limited
47 Water Street, Lavenham, Suffolk CO10 9RN
Telephone 01787 247436
www.lavenhampress.co.uk

Sir Peter Blake

Work in progress from *Under Milkwood*

3

Captain Cat.

Peter Blake. 2002.

In Butcher Beynon's, Gossamer Beynon, daughter, schoolteacher,
dreaming deep, daintily ferrets under a fluttering hummock
of chicken's feathers in a slaughterhouse that has chintz
curtains and a three-pieced suite, and finds, with no
surprise, a small rough ready man with a bushy tail
winking in a paper carrier.   (page 17)

dream ⑦   Peter Blake. 2002.

1

And the Inspectors of cruelty fly down into mrs Butcher Beynon's
dream to persecute mr Beynon for selling
owlmeat, dogs' eyes, manchop.
mr Beynon, in butcher's bloodied apron, spring-heels down
Coronation street, a finger, not his own, in his mouth.
straightfaced in 'his gunning' sleep he pulls the legs of his dreams and
Hunting on pigback shoots down the wild giblets.
(page 20)

Dreams ①   Peter Blake. 2002.

From where you are, you can hear their dreams. Captain Cat,
the retired blind sea-captain, asleep in his bunk in the
seashelled, ship-in-bottled, shipshape best cabin ~~in the~~
of Schooner House dreams of
never such seas as any that swamped the decks of his
S.S. KIDWELLY bellying over the bedclothes and jellyship-slippery
sucking him down salt deep into the Davy dark where the
fish come biting out and nibble him down to his wishbone,
and the long drowned nuzzle up to him   (page 3)

And in the little pink-eyed cottage next to the undertaker's,
lie, alone, the seventeen snoring gentle stone of Mister Waldo,
rabbitcatcher, barber, herbalist, catdoctor, quack his fat pink
hands, palms up, over the edge of the patchwork quilt, his
boots neat and tidy in the washing-basin, his bowler on a
rail above the bed, a milk stout and a slice of cold
bread putting under the pillow; and dripping in the dark
he dreams of.
This little piggy went to market

(page 9)

Peter Blake 2002

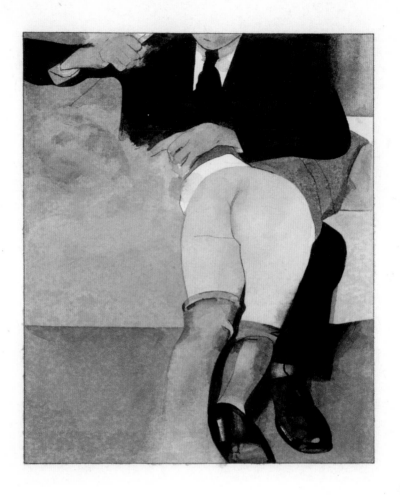

Don't spank me, please, teacher,
whimpers his wife at his side, but every night of her
married life she has been late for school
(page 19)

Peter Blake. 2002.

Alan Brownjohn

The Beacons

Am I hearing them in the dark, reliving the daylight
Of seventy years ago? Her cries of fright
For my safety, in her dread of what she might

See next? Am I feeling now her fury when I made
The opposite kerb untouched? I should have stayed
Till she beckoned me across, but I disobeyed,

Ran out between the studs, saw my face
Staring out at me from a polished space
That brushed my buttons but left no instant trace

On the child inside the blazer, and sped off fast
On its own careless venture.
                    For the last
Ten silent minutes I have seen my past

From tonight's bedroom window, watched the beacons flash
At the crossing, remembered a childhood dash
Which could have proved fatal; resembling my rash

Return to the drink-shelf in a room filled
With the lifelong effects of my not then getting killed,
As if something contradictory in me willed

Both the danger and the safety? Well, I'm still alive…
(And the beacons? Hore-Belisha's, who would survive
To lose his seat in nineteen forty-five.)

On a Birthday

Summer night fallen, and the light outside
Exchanged for a reflection of ourselves
In the café glass, the tannoy playing
Soave sia il vento in the room adjoining
The bakery where earlier they made
The cake on which the candles couldn't be
Lighted because of a somewhere draught from
An open door soon shut to oblige us
– Then the baker's thumb flicked hard on the wheel
Of the lighter again, again, again;
But flames at last so I could blow with closed
Eyes as they swayed and flattened to die out
(And keep my hopes to myself.) Then you said
'You can open them', and I did and saw
The threads of smoke that rose across your smile
As you sang with our reflections smiling
In the July dark, one mile from the dome
Through which we had seen, as they meant us to,
The sky, this day being one week only
Short of an anniversary I'll have
To try to reconcile with a happiness.

Hiroshima 28/7, Café Mozart

Ludbrooke: His Revelation

He becomes aware that it might not be much fun
To be his latest, *the one he really loves*
– His italics, in his email she reads at work.
He recycles the thought in the message he leaves
When he calls her at home that evening, and she is out.
Her cold-voiced message ends, and the promised bleep
Is heard after several seconds, and he begins:
'You must know you are the one I've really *loved*,
And I'm quite aware of how difficult that must be... '
Trailing off in all false modesty. He has a phone
That gives out a wail when he replaces it,
As he does now, on its 'base unit'. He looks at it.
He thinks, 'When I try tactics I know I'm losing.'

Alan Brownjohn's novel *Windows on the Moon*, published in 2009, appears in
paperback in May 2010 and his new book of poems, *Ludbrooke, And Others*,
will be out in July 2010.

Monstrous Men

Nick Sweeney

As a child, I lived in an apartment overlooking K Street, the imperial city centre of pageantry and postcards. Once I'd started music lessons with Mr Z, our music room gradually filled up with tapestries, books and chatchkas. Garden tools and furniture were added, then dressers and beds and wardrobes. I saw that our country house now occupied the room.

Our servants had vanished. By that time, kings were shot in basements, dukes slaved as waiters, princesses danced in shows, and prime ministers' heads were sent around the country in biscuit tins; people went out for a newspaper, and never came back.

Mr Z complained, 'This … *junk* ruins the acoustics.' I nearly had one of my legendary tantrums; that was our country house he was talking about, a life we would no longer lead.

One day he brought a small guitar, looted, he claimed, when he fought during the Great War, from the apartment of an Irish writer who had lived in Trieste.

After lessons, Mr Z ate supper and gushed about the arts to my parents, who were mystified by art of any kind. They only encouraged me to play because my character, defined by petulance and whim, fitted me for no practical subjects.

On my eleventh birthday Mr Z barked, 'You will never be a musician,' and rapped my knuckles with his baton. He should have stayed for supper that night, because he blundered into a riot on K Street, by then a focus for rioters, and was killed with a spade, of all things.

I practised as if he were still at my side. With the light off, I was able to play without looking, emulating Mr Z's blindness, which was the other thing he brought back from that war.

The invitation to view the latest work by celebrated painter LM came to my classroom one day as I got my eleven-year-olds to clap, which was my method prior to letting them loose on instruments. The bearer stepped to my desk, saying, 'I will relay your reply.'

'Relay?' I knew him from the Eagle Café, his habitual seat beneath our president's portrait. He had the secret policeman look; not just the drab clothes, more the watchfulness, the look of a man who wore glasses but had forgotten them. I said, 'Certainly, Hermes.'

'Hermes?' He looked puzzled.

L's painting was called *The Father of My Child*. Her invitation brought up images I rarely recalled. She used to gaze out of windows opposite mine on K Street, and we exchanged glances as nannies coincided us in and out. Soon after the nannies disappeared, my father had gone out for a newspaper into a place nobody knew, and I had moved away, to the suburbs.

L and I met again in our twenties, loafed in cafés and exchanged glances that led into an affair punctuated by arguments about art, political compromise and duty. Over the years since, I had run into her occasionally, L slipping barbs into our banter to address any of my failings that she had thought of since our liaison.

L's child, I knew, was dark-eyed and scrawny, with thick black hair, and she brooded; in all those attributes, she was like me.

People whispered that L was the president's lover, then had to add hastily that he loved us all. It was L who had painted his portrait, which hung in every workplace, his eyes eerily following those of his people. L's studio was on top of one wing of the presidential palace. I read the title of her new work again, and had to restrain myself from gazing up at the portrait over my blackboard.

The children were clapping in seven-eight time, and I saw that our visitor was unsettled by it. It is cacophonous if there is even one child slightly out. There always is.

On the invitation, L had scrawled, *You MUST bring your genial child musicians to play our song. RSVP in the affirmative.*

Our song was called *Quaintrelle's Chorus*, and L believed I had written it for her. That was just a lover's lie. I had simply chosen it from a collection of manuscripts I kept locked up. The children's seven-eight clapping prompted my recall of its finer details.

'Your answer?' Hermes had really had enough.

'Tell Madam it will be a pleasure.' I walked him to the door. 'Where are your glasses?'

'Glasses?' He blinked.

'And your wings?'

'Wings? What do you mean?'

'You.' I looked urbane and worldly, I thought, in my linen suit, and my canvas oxfords. And him in his serge, and his gabardine, his stupid hat. 'Hermes.'

At the door, he switched off the light. 'Not time yet for the lights.' He wagged a finger at the clock. 'Every gram of energy saved – remember?'

Perhaps he expected me to finish the propaganda ministry's slogan. I just smiled, worldly, urbane.

'How can you stand this? ' He meant the clapping, which was at a beautiful, and transient, point; it would get no better. I refrained from the retort, *And how can you stand beating people in cells?* Perhaps he sensed the question. He glanced up at the portrait of his master, and I saw his face compose itself, happy to be that of his official business again.

In my early twenties, I motored around the countryside at weekends. One day I was on a deserted road when the engine gave out. I walked in hope of help towards the next village.

I gradually noticed red cloths tied into hedges, perhaps every half-kilometre. At a fork in the road, the cloth pointed away from the village, but I followed it all the same.

A Gypsy came to meet me. When he had made up his mind that I wasn't an official of some kind, he invited me to his camp, up a barely navigable track signalled by two lots of red cloth.

'You mark the path,' I observed. He denied it. 'Yes,' I went on, excited at my smartness, 'you hide it and show it all at once.'

'No.'

'That,' I marvelled, 'is … genius.'

I was depressed by his command not to mention that I had spotted the signs; one thing I loved about the countryside was people's openness, unlike in the cities, where we went about our business without catching the eye of another person in case we made an enemy of them, suspecting ourselves of things we were never sure of.

At the camp there were perhaps twenty Gypsies, all ages from ninety to nine months. A youth was deputised to ride a horse up the road and look at my car. As I ate with them, they unravelled stories that formed such a perfect picture of Gypsy life that I sensed it was all made up, but I appreciated it anyway.

They were clearing out a wagon so that they could set up an oven to fashion an order of copper pans for a local landowner. Among the items displaced from the wagon was a wooden box containing, I saw with astonishment, handwritten music. I asked if I could see it, and my guide bade me examine it.

I picked up the first sheet. The writing was that of one of those composers who visited country people, transcribing their music for posterity. I had seen some of it in the ethnographic museum. I was about to exclaim, *That's B's music*, when guile shut me up.

'Where did you get this?' I asked, and I sensed another tale about to begin, but before it could get going my guide signalled for silence.

'Can any of you play it?' I wondered, and they laughed.

'We have no use for it.' The guide indicated the oven.

I said, 'Then why don't you give it to … musical Gypsies?' I had seen them at country weddings; with unsettling expertise, they held the music on the brink of chaos but never let it go there.

The guide said, 'Bad blood between us at the moment.'

I hummed the tune of a piece in eleven-eight, and somebody shouted bravo. Then they clapped the strange rhythm and closed in, faces bright with the joy of making noise.

'Can I buy it from you?' My question was the one towards which we had all been heading. As the others left us to it, my guide sucked in his breath.

'It has great sentimental value for us,' he said.

'Of course.' I'd just seen perfect tunes whose authors were long dead, along with the transcribing composer, and I imagined the glory that would fall on my head when I revealed those melodies to the world. 'I'm sure it has.'

'And you can't put a price on that.' The guide put an arm around my shoulder. 'Usually.'

In the week before L's unveiling, I filtered its soundtrack through my insomnia. I stood on my balcony during a storm, heard the birds in the trees on the square chirping diminished chords, imagined them cursed with the faces of the genius children L wanted to play at her *concerto de camera*.

To do *Quaintrelle's Chorus* the full gothic justice it deserved, I saw, it needed wind and brass. Over several café breakfasts, ignoring the myopic Hermes in his corner, I arranged it over a percussion part using only handclaps.

'How easily your art vanishes,' L had been fond of saying. 'Stop listening, and it's gone.'

I would counter, 'Well, you can burn a canvas.' I had already lost the argument, because L only painted onto walls; foundries, factories, museums, opera houses. To suggest bombs and bulldozers would have been sedition.

Quaintrelle's Chorus came into my head the night L and I broke up. I remembered the day I exchanged it for the car.

'I don't expect men to change just for me,' L was saying. She looked beautiful, and insane, and weary of me. We were about to have a conversation that, a year earlier, might have broken my heart. By then I was glad of it. 'What I *do* expect is for them to regret not changing, later on.'

'I'm sure they'll let you know as soon as that happens.' I laughed.

Betraying a momentary falter, L said, 'You're mocking me.'

'Yes,' I admitted.

She said, '*Yes* is a great last word to have.'

'Is it, L?'

'Yes.'

L was not going to get geniuses for her unveiling. My talented but jaded sixteen-year-olds, I decided, would ruin the song by rendering it perfectly. No, eleven was the age to be for that mix of sweetness to the edge of chaos; after eleven they would be distracted, and ruined, by hormones and ideologies, the intricacies of rifles and childbirth. My eleven-year-olds were the real genii, and we would work magic.

On the night of the unveiling, we left the presidential guardians who met us at the palace's servants' entrance staring, dismayed, at our invitation as we shoved our way through corridors in a flurry of Babel and instrument cases.

The tastelessness of the main hall awed me into silence: hanging in alcoves like game trophies were icons of murdered soldiers and politicians, the president's one-time friends. The surroundings were meant to inspire silence, but silence cannot be worked onto eleven-year-olds. In a raucous confusion, we descended on the stage area, and began unpacking and tuning.

'Where is N?' I asked, struck suddenly by the absence of a dumpy, freckled kid with honey-coloured hair and obsessive green eyes; her clarinet was to have soared, or, in her case, barged, in and out of the second verse. Nobody knew or cared where N was, apart from the panicked flautist I deputised to play her part.

'Where is the audience?' a child asked. It was a better question.

'The musicians always arrive early,' I assured her, but sensed our audience around us, eyes following us from the walls, like those of the president in that wretched portrait with which L had cursed us all.

But where was the artist, and who was the father of her child? The answer lay behind a curtain across the room. I resisted the urge to wander over and peek.

The audience entered. It was a group of functionaries in suits and uniforms, and at the sight of us they stopped, confused. In the midst of them shambled a wild-eyed man, unshaven and unkempt, our president.

My musicians stood and yelled, 'Greetings, our president,' the way the etiquette handbook had instructed. I begrudged it; it was his place, and he should have been greeting *us*.

Our glorious leader resembled a barbarian who had just been roused. But above all, he looked anguished at the sight of us all. He beckoned an aide, who beckoned another, and they had a discussion culminating in a stare across the room to the man I knew as Hermes.

I was distracted by L's entry, behind the audience. She started gracefully, but then her posture became combative when she saw the empty chairs. She sent an impatient look towards us, and shouted, 'Play!'

And, concentrated, my genii ignored their conductor and stuttered into musical momentum. I was too busy watching the cabaret out in the audience.

The palace factota were hesitant. None of them caught L as she stepped to the curtain guarding her picture, and wrapped the cord around her wrist. Declaiming the title over and over, she pulled. The masterpiece was simply a giant rendition, on the palace wall, of the portrait we saw everywhere. There were some differences: he was wearing a tatty brocaded gown much like the one worn by the living, seething president, and he looked much like the man we saw; wizened, mean, dull-eyed, corrupted by his own invincibility.

The music and clapping touched the verge of perfection. The functionaries advanced on us. The last thing I saw was the face of Hermes as, my arms gripped from behind by one of his colleagues, he pressed his thumbs into my eyes and expertly turned them in their sockets, a second's work to put my lights out forever.

★

I love the way Parisians keep their air of liberty, even if equality and fraternity may be sadly lacking. They make it clear that they don't like me stealing their thunder in concert halls, or teaching their morose children at the Conservatory. But as long as I don't overdraw at the bank, or slight any of their dignitaries at receptions, I am now, and forever, one of them.

My apartment overlooks the Batignolles Park, said to be beautiful. Probably, it's just a park, variegated in spring and autumn, green in summer, white in winter, full of dog-walking dames, starchy nannies and crow-like concierges.

N described it for me all the same. She was the child who feigned sickness on the evening of L's unveiling to cover her ineptitude on the clarinet: a genuine stroke of genius. At the age of twenty-five, she had wriggled under that Iron Curtain and made her way to Paris, and to me, to be my eyes, and the source of all my comforts.

One night at a recital I was giving, it was whispered during the interval that a lady from my country was in the audience, a real one in lace and pearls. But any roaming Romanov or hapless Habsburg with a scratchy voice was said to be from my country. When she was shown into my dressing room, she was revealed as no lady, but émigré artist LM.

The first time L called on me, N left me to remind L of the evening her crazy lover ordered the blinding of the artist, the conductor and the orchestra, N's unfortunate classmates. It wasn't long before L was wailing, 'I spent my life loving monstrous men.' I brought this particular drama to a close by asking about L's child.

'She was dull, and untalented,' L began.

'Oh.' I knew then that she couldn't be mine, and was pleased. 'But … what happened to her?'

As a child of privilege, she'd been allowed anywhere she wanted to go. This included the cages at the palace zoo where, one day, a gibbon bit her. The wound festered, and she died, closely followed, probably, by the monkey keeper and the nanny.

'Were you sad?' I wondered.

'She was my child,' L snapped. 'People close to you don't have to be perfect for you to miss them. You're not perfect. I missed you.'

When she moved in, L insisted that N should go. She was right; I had sensed for a while that it was long past time for her to be among her own kind, the sighted, the young; I had been feeling like a jailer. She was replaced by a rotund Romany woman called J.

'The blind leading the blind,' L became fond of saying, 'led in front by the drab.'

But I liked the sense that J brought to our lives. One morning J told us about the cheerful vagabondage of her people in France, how they made their dark children and their bright pots and cloth flowers and played a gothic kind of guitar jazz, stole the swans from the parks to eat. I told her about the Gypsies I met, of their stories and their food and their fire, and about their red threads in the hedges, and she dismissed them thus: 'Coppersmiths, they never laugh.' True, I couldn't recall any of them laughing. But who had anything to laugh about in those times, and in that country of mine, except me, clutching my contraband music?

L dismissed J, bade her go laundering or marketing.

She waited for a minute or so, then, said, 'Remember we used to live up this high?' Even if your legs had forgotten the stairs, you sensed the height. She prompted, 'When we were young?'

'Yes.' I hadn't thought of the apartment on K Street for a long time.

'I used to watch you.'

'I know.'

'I remember your music lessons.'

'Oh? Well, I remember you painting.' I thought I did, anyway.

'What about your last lesson?'

'What about it?' I remembered the claustrophobia and the clutter. I recalled a trace of quinine on Mr Z's breath, rusting buttons on his jacket.

'What did your teacher do to you,' L asked gently, 'that made you run to the window, watch the street and wait for him, and impale the poor man with a garden spade?'

I remembered that, too. The pause I made had gone on long enough when I said, 'I just wanted to frighten him.'

L was silent, but I had to assume she was about to ask why.

'He told me I'd never be a musician.' It was a lame excuse for an act with such an unfortunate ending. 'And that was all I wanted to be. When he told me that, I never felt so frightened in my life. I wanted him to feel frightened too.'

And so he had, but not by me. I saw his slight figure again, his hesitation when he heard the crowd filling the street, the shouting, the breaking of glass and the thump of stones. He dropped his cane, and lurched away from the wall to find it, leading him into the path of the spade, which I'd meant only to clatter next to him.

'Monstrous men,' L said softly. 'I spent my life loving monstrous men.'

I couldn't argue with her. I pondered the kindnesses I'd tried to do throughout my life; they worked, but were all somehow solipsistic.

'You only wanted to frighten him,' L accepted. 'It was a child's wish.'

'And children are monstrous.' I remembered them all, my genii, the spontaneous cruelty in their everyday gestures and words, but it wasn't the real cruelty they would have learned, had they grown up with their eyes about them. 'Without really meaning it.'

'Anyway, look at you.' L laughed, slapped my knee. 'Here you are, carrying on Mr Z's good work, and carrying his white stick.'

I had often recalled Hermes in the Eagle Café, sipping his coffee under L's portrait of his master. I could never get a picture of his whole face, just his eyes, anxious, exposed, whereas it was my eyes that were exposed, by his fingers, for the last time. L told me he was killed by precipitation from the top of the palace, not for mislaying his glasses, but for forgetting to cancel the musicians, once the president's agents had discovered L's ridiculous plan to show the world the father of her child. He could have done with some wings, then. When L told me that, I realised that I had never been able to picture him properly because I had been seeking a picture of another monstrous man, when I should have been searching for the blinking, genial face of a child.

Nick Sweeney divides his time between writing prose and music these days. He can sometimes be seen in the guise of a Russian sailor in the burlesque, Balkan world of the Trans-Siberian March Band – see www.tsmb.co.uk.

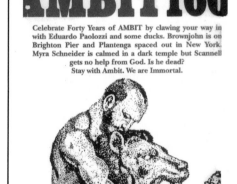

Martin Cook

Ariadne's Escape

Had Theseus not scrambled his brains
in fights with giants, ogres and bandits,
he'd never have volunteered
to challenge the minotaur.

Ariadne's nimble fingers were skilled
in the arts of embroidery and tapestry,
and she used twine to ensure she came home
safe from the darkest tunnels.

She took a clew to help the man
her eyes had longingly caressed,
hoping for recompense in his arms,
when he'd slain the beast
and freed his compatriots.

Later, she clung to him, a limpet
and his bawdy crew mocked –
so he abandoned her on Naxos,
where she met and married
the merriest of gods, Dionysus.

Jumping to Conclusions

Blood on a lion's paws
does not always mean a kill;
perhaps an acacia thorn
penetrated between pads;
perhaps blood's been spilt
competing for a lioness.

Dark stains in dust
on a shadowy jungle path
through the Anamallai Hills
do not always mean
a chital or ibex wounded
by an incompetent poacher.

A Tamil, spitting betel juice,
makes the same dark splash
on mottled Kadar tracks
through the bamboo belt,
where king cobras watch
for unwary rat snakes
and swallow them without
one drop of gore or fluid.

Notes: Kadar – A jungle tribe in the Anamallai Hills,
Tamil Nadu. King cobras – There is a nature reserve
for them in the hills.

Enkidu Speaks

Mark my words, Gilgamesh,
and whatever I say
may seem like trash to you;
your puny peasants are ants,
fed on cultured grasses –
they do whatever you
or your fawning cronies say.

You despise me as wild,
unkempt, unschooled
in sophisticated small talk
and without knowledge
of your silly legends
of Utnapishtim and Humbaba.

I've no need for any
of that twaddle, for I've
the wind in my hair
and sun on my back
between dawn and sunset.
I eat fruits of the land
and thank the flesh I eat.

You also feed well, but
exhaust the land to provide
grain for your minions,
who mean nothing to you
unless they slave to raise ziggurats
or bring chained folk to sacrifice
to bloodthirsty Marduck.

Know this, Gilgamesh,
although I'm no prophet
and lack book-learning,
I see envy among scrawny peons
and wonder how long
the walls of Erech and Ur will stand.

Martin Cook was born in India in 1937. His butterfly career has included soldiering, tea planting, marketing and social services. His poems have appeared in a variety of magazines including *Acumen*, *Agenda*, *Ambit*, *Magma* and *The Rialto*. His first collection, *Mackerel Wrappers*, is published by Happenstance.

Reviews

Blood / Sugar
James Byrne
Arc £9.99

I liked this collection best when I read it backwards. That is to say when I started with the Notes pages (which I welcomed) and went in reverse order. There is a reason for this, about which I shall come clean.

If you start at the front, the first poem is 'Recovery', a lyric in two-line stanzas which demonstrates beautifully how aware Byrne is of the dramatic intensity commanded by delaying impact, by stretching sentences to their limit, by working the white space:

There are dinner-halls you have silenced
with a single spark of wit,

there are men you have governed
through pure scent, pure posture.

I start to be less comfortable on the next page when the white space gets bigger, ellipses appear in little clumps (sometimes inside brackets) and asterisks invade. Asterisks do something to my sensibility I don't like. If I were at school, I would be the kid making a venomous hole with the point of my pencil through every evil asterisk. This reaction is neither rational nor helpful.

So let me recommence at the back of the book, where the asterisks take longer to appear or are less intrusive. I am fine with the modestly asterisky 'Thieves' Society', for example: the language is gorgeously dressed:

In Garry bars the once-ambrosial. Rounds of
*   Happyslap. Hophead.*
Stick in the gullet blade. Two taps to bald the
*   face of a kitchen window.*
The boiler suit fits all. The foursquare room
*   with a chain-bit libbard.*

It is 'Doctor One-Eye' before there is serious asterisk invasion, and although I don't really understand this poem, I'm desensitized by now. I'm clocking the fact that this is intelligent stuff, lots of allusions, some humour, playfulness and – hey – not all my cup of tea but I like enough to make me think this man

repays proper scrutiny. I think 'Avoiding a Close Reading of Geoffrey Hill's Mercian Hymns' is excellent; and I like 'The Ashes' and 'Entry (Cornwall 1991)' a lot. I don't subscribe to the blurb on the back cover, which suggests I should be knocked off my chair by Byrne as 'phenomenon', but he has my attention. He has my attention…
Helena Nelson

Giraffe under a Grey Sky
Danielle Hope
Rockingham Press £7.99

The cover put me off this book. That giraffe has a tacky look to it, especially under the bold blue italicized book title. I was relieved to find the contents subtler than I expected. The title poem ('Giraffe') is nicely surreal and several other poems also come neatly at a subject from an off-the-wall perspective. The poet is enjoying herself, I think. Many of these texts would do well in public reading. In fact, while a few feel slight on the page, I suspect they would all perform well.

The 'Mrs Uomo' sequence sits at the heart of the book. There are seven poems about her and I liked her. Mrs Uomo is both bizarre and ordinary at the same time. She develops through the sequence and she has charm: I particularly liked the way she keeps her regrets in a corner cover and 'lifts them out piece by piece / delicate as bone china'. She longs to bundle them all in a bin bag and give them to charity but

[…] while she wishes a new regret takes shape
in her hand. So Mrs Uomo polishes it
then puts it up on the shelf.

This is a poet who spans octaves of tone – from whimsical to cheery to plangent – and she clearly delights in the contrast. I will not easily forget the brutally businesslike register of 'Request', which draws no conclusions and leaves the reader to choose between terminating life (with dignity) or extending it at any cost:

She was 42, and he 83. And you?
Not ready to dispense magic potions of polar
*   kinds,*
not yet believing in lottery tickets, treasure finds
lucky charms and all newspaper headlines?

Helena Nelson

Two For Joy: Scenes from Married Life
Dannie Abse
Hutchinson £15

I feel as though I've been reading Dannie Abse all my life. He's been there as long as I can remember, a sane, reassuring, measured voice in the midst of much mayhem. When I heard his wife had been killed in a car crash in 2005, the pang I felt was unusually deep, although I had only ever met him through two slight and battered volumes of his work. The rest of my acquaintance rested on magazines here and there over the years.

So how could I have forgotten 'Epithalamion', which is in my *Selected* and reappears here? How could I have thought I appreciated old Abse faithfully and appropriately, like a comfy chair or a traditional garden? There is nothing ordinary in this volume with Abse's wife Joan at the heart of it. It is beautiful. It is moving. The command of cadence and phrasing is unerring: more than once it moved me to tears.

It is not a bleak book, even though its theme is loss. It made me envious: how remarkable to have had this relationship, to be haunted by its life-enhancing resonance. Of course, there is darkness. Abse is a realist and hides nothing. Even in 'Verses at Night', before anything dreadful has happened, his apprehensive cry is the voice of our common fear in the face of dread:

'No,' I cry as by her side I sprawl.
'No,' impotently, as I hear my small
dear daughter whimper in her cot
and across the darkness call.

These are poems that both sing and think. They reflect on themselves. In 'Postscript', the final poem in the set, the poet asks:

So though late, all too late, is it demeaning
to publish love lyrics about you now?

Many a muse has exercised her power in absence. This address to a wife, across a barrier none can cross, invests language with urgent irony. What is the meaning of life? And death – what does it mean? And what does poetry 'mean'? Does death de-mean? Can Love itself – after death – give meaning?

Well, yes. I think it can and the proof is here:

It's when I'm most myself, most alone
with all the clamour of my senses dumb,
then, in the confusion of Time's deletion
by Eternity, I welcome you and you return
improbably close, though of course you cannot
come.

Helena Nelson

Later Selected Poems
Sheenagh Pugh
Seren £9.99

This is a truly enjoyable collection. I was savouring it in such a relaxed and self-indulgent way at the hairdresser's last December – rehearsing various phrases and narrative threads in my mind while my hair was being coloured and snipped – that my mindstate became far too reflective and relaxed.

That's how the book got left behind in the middle of curlers and potions and scissors and why the review did not get written for the last issue of *Ambit*. I did not write about the haunting character of Lieutenant Hans Hermann von Katte, whose awful death in 1730 haunted me and does so still, nor the noble Lady Jane Franklin, who first refused to accept her husband's death in the Arctic and later mourned him so plangently:

I am not sure anyone would believe
in him now, but I knew him, and he died
on June the eleventh, eighteen-forty-seven,
and whoever was near him, I was not.

Later Selected Poems was twenty-five miles away in a hairdresser's cupboard, but these words followed me around until I repossessed the volume and the personages inside it like long-lost friends.

And no wonder: the book is rich in narrative and emotion. Often (but by no means always) Pugh writes in persona, or in sequences which move from voice to voice. The mind-states she commands in this way have great poignancy: the person who believes in the Windfarm Angels and 'their white embrace'; the lover in 'Alternate' who knows (and aches to know) his love-making is simply a script, into which his woman can write her preferred partner; the 'Thief of Love' who breaks in as 'chancer, levanter / and picklock'.

Pugh is accomplished in many methods and styles. Occasionally an individual poem struck me as strong in style but slight in matter. As soon as I caught myself thinking that, however, another would capture me with unusual intensity. So much so that I am inclined to think variety in itself lends this collection a particular attraction. Different people will have different favourites but it's hard to believe anyone could take up this book and not be absorbed and enriched. *Helena Nelson*

Life is a Dream: 40 Years Reading Poems 1967–2007
Paul Duncan
Harvill Secker £16.99

The first Durcan poem I ever read was 'The Arnolfini Marriage': it was in an educational publication accompanied by the famous painting which inspired it. I liked it back then and I liked making its acquaintance once more in this handsome forty-years-worth-of-poems book. In fact, I liked several of the poems from the *Give Me Your Hand* (1994) section, particularly 'Mr and Mrs Andrews' ('after Thomas Gainsborough'). It's witty and wry and Durcan uses the persona 'voice' beautifully – it is one of his distinctive skills.

Which was just as well, because my second meeting with Durcan was *The Art of Life* (2004), which did little for me, and I felt no different on second meeting in this volume. It occurred to me that this was perhaps because I had no sense of the poet's human voice. In fact, I may well be one of the few poetry lovers who has managed not to hear Durcan live (though also one of the select number who has read this *Collected* volume carefully from beginning to end). According to his Foreword the poet thinks live readings are crucial.

I was sure I could remedy this omission by consulting the National Poetry Archive website, but Durcan was not there. I tracked him down on Youtube, Ottawa International Writers Festival 2009 (49 views). Watching and hearing him at last, I observed that many of his poems are not dissimilar to the narrative links with which poets often entertain their audiences between poems: genial anecdotes, reflections on personal experience offered with charm. That is certainly part of his art

(though by no means all) and I think there are instances of it working effectively: monologues where I liked the voice; I liked the sometimes surreal oddness of events very much; I liked the humour.

I thought he got prosier with the turn of the century; prosier, more sprawly and less stimulating. The concluding poem in this volume (which I take to be an important piece for Durcan, 'My Mother's Secret') begins:

Like all women of her generation
My mother had a secret,
Which was that as a young woman
In Paris in the 1930s
She had played the oboe...

This is as near to conversational prose as poetry gets.

To find Durcan at his best, I turn to the angry political poems like 'Oagh' and 'Ken Saro-Wiwa Park' and 'The Bloomsday Murders, 16 June 1997'. These are pitched so much higher: they assert themselves absolutely. Equally I admire the way Durcan draws on a musical tradition through repetition and cadence (some of the prosy poems build towards lines of gorgeous aural resonance). But I like his ballad self best. 'My Bride of Aherlow', from *Cries of an Irish Caveman* (2001), is the one I would be taking to a desert island. I swear I can hear his voice in it, each rhythmic step sure and clear, and a voice older than his singing through it. It will outlive him. *Helena Nelson, Jim Burns*

Tigers at Awhitu
Sarah Broom
Carcanet £9.95

Weather, countryside and surroundings act as a catalyst throughout much of the poetry in Sarah Broom's first collection, although at times I felt there were too many divergences from this strong theme. New Zealand's landscape is strong throughout her poems as well as being apparent in the title – Awhitu is a peninsula in New Zealand that is steeped in Maouri history.

The first poem 'Snow' is an excellent beginning, paving the way for a strong collaboration between the natural world, human nature and the feeling of insignificance when faced with the unpredictability of life. Broom portrays a real sense of environment and humanity co-habiting: each intrinsic to the other:

It was as the snow started falling again
that she blurted it out…the news that slipped
out like a necklace from a sleeve,
not meant for the kids, not meant for here

The 'here' is central to several of the poems in *Tigers at Awhitu*; 'here' is the setting of each poem, the place and atmosphere where the action happens. Broom makes the relation-ship between catastrophe and place a vital one. This is seen again in 'Under the Hospital' where Broom beautifully uses the outside to represent the inside. We see a person in an underground car park, underneath the hospi-tal before visiting a patient.

I can feel the impossible weight of the hospital
pressing down on the concrete ceiling: the beds,
the oxygen machines, the laundry bags, bins

The oppression of the hospital is created so tangibly, we can feel the reluctance and resignation the visitor feels.

A strong theme can focus a collection, but after a while the poems moved away from the inherent connection between emotion, the action and its setting which was a little disap-pointing. That said the individual poems are robust. Motherhood, children and nature are of the utmost importance to Broom and are all explored in poems such as 'This Space', 'Spring' and 'Husk'. It is the poems which transport the reader to the stories of Esau and Jacob in 'Twins' and which look at the rules and traditions written for priests to follow in 'Leviticus' that really stand out:

I took my two doves and two pigeons
For the priest, and as he killed them neatly
For the offering – one burnt offering, one sin
offering –
I thought about how clean she was when she
was born

The confusion of a mother who sees her new-born as cleaner and purer than any existing thing is beautifully composed.

Broom's talent emerges most when writ-ing of her passions and experiences and the intensity of these poems counterbalances any weakness in overall theme of this collection.
Daisy Bowie-Sell

Visiting Exile
John Welch
Shearsman £8.95

Earl's Court, the evening heat
Stretched out between the terraces
Where tourists pitch their tents.
Walking as if to nowhere in particular
This crowd has learned to look and eat and
travel
All in the one movement.

I've taken those lines from one of John Welch's poems because they seem to typify his way of writing. He doesn't go in for straightforward descriptions of city life but instead aims for what might almost appear to be a fragmentary style in which images and ideas are juxtaposed so as to set up a tension. And perhaps that's an effective way of dealing with the city and its diversities.

Welch had many years experience of working as a teacher in multicultural educa-tion in an inner city environment, and quite a few of his poems reflect that fact. They also pick up on aspects of London's imperialist past and of events in India. A longish piece, 'Lyrical Cities', neatly combines several of these influences. It kicks off with lines by a nineteenth-century Iraqi poet who was in Delhi at the time of the Indian Mutiny, brings in a few original lines by John Welch, uses an anecdote about a schoolboy from Lahore in a school in East London, and ends with more from Welch:

Look up – a faint screaming,
Yes those are swifts
Making their sky meal
And the inward fortifications?

Well, I had made myself lonely.

It's worth noting that Welch appends a page of notes to this poem and that, together with its piecemeal (as some might see it) approach, could cause a few readers to ask if a poem ought to be constructed in that way and require explanation. Welch doesn't write easy poems, in the sense of their being immedi-ately understandable, but there is something in his work worth searching for.
Jim Burns

A. A. Marcoff

Creation

In the beginning the earth was the song of a virgin
empty for an age:
her womb was of bamboo & water
& her hair was the wind in the trees:
here eyes were as day & night
the left & the right
& her breasts were as mountains
of bright fertile rock:
she sang & she sang & she sang
of fishes & turtles
whales & sea-horses bearing shells of desire:

And the melody of earth grew substantial:
time took shape with her song
& energised her deepest breath
to bring more light to her ravenous womb:

And at the hour of the wolf
(the gap between night & dawn)
her children emerged of music –
airborn
& pregnant with time again
she sang to them of love:
& her children grew through the stars that were their eyes
& bamboo & water
permeated the land
& the hair of her head
spread across the mountains
& she sang song after song
that turned dust into diamonds
& ashes into birds:

And the rocks are alight with the tongues of living fire
that speak of light to the holograph of darkness:
sing out of the light!
sing out of the dark!

And the tongues of the rocks call the wild horses
to carry men into the mountains of light
& to bring the tongues of living fire
into the minds of the free:

And in every tongue there is an avalanche
of wild white words suffused with heat
& as a token of the visions to come with eyes
the heart of rock will simply learn to beat:
the great holograph of darkness is lit up by gems that speak

Equus

Have you heard about that doctor's nightmare
        and his vision of the horses' heads?
Have you heard the holy snarls
        or seen the dark flared nostrils
        as six horses reared up high
        into
            the nebula
of the dream?

Do you know the genesis of religion,
        as the boy discarded
saddle, shackle, leather, reins?

The horses run wild there,
            out in the grounds
of mind,
        shining like the sea.

And it started with a picture on the wall,
            above the boy's bed,
as the image of a horse
        merged perfectly
with scripture, becoming God.

And it led to that nocturnal rite of ecstasy,
        the boy naked on the horse,
both sweating in their deep communion,
        haunch to haunch,
        roaming the fields,
the trees a dark curtain
behind.

And the language of his liturgy was boyish all right,
complete with a genealogy some would call grotesque.
Do you call it the power of the horseshoe
or that of the horse's eye?

'Equus! Equus!'
He calls.
And the doctor sits slouched over his desk at night
        in deep vision
disturbed by the horses' heads,
        there
in the grounds
of mind,
shining
        like the sea.

'O Equus, do you gallop the world freely now
        with moonlit winds
            in your mane,
or do you draw the mind of Man
        into your huge eyes,
jealously as the god
        conjured
out of pictures of the centaur?'

And the doctor remains at his desk,
and he listens to the power
        of hooves
in the grounds of his mind.

And he hears a boy –
    who blinds six horses
    with a metal spike –
    screaming:-

  'Then Equus see no more!'

And the doctor sighs,

  'Alas, Equus, you still see me.'

A. A. Marcoff is an Anglo-Russian poet, born in Iran. He has lived in Africa, Iran,
France and Japan. A regular contributor to the haiku magazines, he has had longer
work appear in *Poetry Review*, *Agenda*, *Fire* and *Acumen*. He lives by the beautiful
River Mole in Surrey.

The Forest of Veils

Douglas Thompson

I think we are in rats' alley
where the dead men lost their bones.

'What is that noise?'
　　　The wind under the door.

T. S. Eliot, *The Waste Land*

Vittorrio and Lucia cowered beneath the blankets as the night wind raged outside, the noise merging threateningly with the raised voices of their parents arguing in the next room.

The wind seemed to be harrying fences, billowing trees, bending creaking branches to breaking point. In Vittorrio's mind the wind and the night were like one entity now, fused as waves of some nocturnal ocean that was sweeping and engulfing the whole city, testing everything in its path.

The argument in the next room made no more sense to him than the angry sounds outside, blind rage, pleading indignation, sighing despair. What would be left standing in the morning? Who would make sense of the debris, pick out what fragments were salvageable and make repairs?

With one eye open beneath the covers, Vittorrio caught sight of his posters in the moonlight on the opposite wall: Aztec and Inca cities, *Pompeii, Angkor Wat*... obviously sometimes things were not always well again in the morning. Logically such a time had to come for some people, when on an arbitrary whim their lives were just totally wrecked by the untrammelled forces of nature. Then they just packed up and walked away from it all to become nomadic hunter gatherers again. History was littered with the ruins they had left behind each time it happened, all those archaeological digs. Was it lack of resources or lack of heart that turned them away in the end, unable to face the rebuilding? Vittorrio decided to ask his father some of these questions in the morning, if the house was still standing.

★

And I don't want that witch anywhere inside this house while I'm away… Claudia sighed bitterly, shaking her head from side to side as she spoke, her hands in her hair, eyes downcast to the floor.

Franco stood at the window with his back turned, staring out into the raging night as if it was some inscrutable puzzle he could unlock with a skilful glance.

I understand, he mumbled gruffly.

But do you? Claudia came back, head forward like a bird of prey. *I don't want her anywhere near the children,* Our *children, you understand?*

Of course, he said, sighing, and returning to sit down facing her, taking his glasses off.

You silly old fool… she muttered harshly as she looked again at his vulnerability, the half-blind eyes, his baby-soft cheeks.

I'm the same age as you… he replied rather lamely.

Yes, Franco, old in today's youth-obsessed culture, past it. Don't you see that this silly little tart is just playing with you? Wrecking your life, our marriage, for a laugh?

He started to shake his head then put his glasses back on and nodded: *I admit the possibility…*

And you'll expect me to take you back after all that? After you're the laughing stock of the whole town?

I expect nothing, he replied grimly, *not from you, nor from the creator of the universe. This is just what it is, the situation, I make no excuses.*

You realise I will leave you when I return if you haven't sorted yourself out…if you haven't got her out of your life?

He nodded his head silently.

We're not going to be one of those weird couples with an OPEN RELATIONSHIP Franco, you might want to live like a freak but I certainly won't.

I'm not turning into a freak or a hippie, Claudia, let's not be childish. This is a calamity, something that has hit me, hit this marriage out of the blue, and now I am trying to understand it, to come to terms with it, find a solution and find how to move forward.

Ah-huh…and will this search for a solution involve you fucking her again, do you think?

Claudia… Franco sighed in despair, *I hate hearing you use language like that, it's horrible, it's not like you…*

Oh really? And what is like me? What the hell do you really know about me after all these years? What is the correct language for a situation like this? Swahili? Esperanto? I'll bet she uses a lot more colourful language than me. So answer the question, will you be fucking her, Franco?

★

The older you get the less coincidences surprise you. Three days before her pre-arranged holiday with Vivienne, Claudia ran into Anton in the street. Or rather, Lucia spotted him among the crowds on Market Street and trotted over to him and said: *Hello, you saved my brother, you brought him back. Are you an angel? Please come and see my mother, please save her next…please come.*

Claudia was hiding her sleepless eyes behind her dark glasses when she realised she had momentarily lost sight of Lucia. She looked around startled and then like the answer to an unasked question: Lucia emerged from the crowd leading Anton by the hand. She recognised his face, failed to remember for a moment who exactly he was, unlike her daughter.

Mrs Reinwald... Anton began and reached out his hand, squinting to see past her glasses and verify her identity. She put her hand up to her hair self-consciously as she took her glasses off, concerned it would be obvious that she had been crying recently.

It's Anton, he explained, to save her embarrassment, *Anton Perlato, I found your son when he went missing*, and he smiled, turning to look at Vittorrio who was holding her other hand.

For a moment she was overwhelmed by the strangeness of the scene, like they were a surrogate family together, as if her whole life had taken an instant and oblique shift sideways.

Anton seemed to read this, and carefully returned Lucia to her other hand, all the time watching her eyes, as if he were carefully adjusting the balance in an artistic composition, a still-life with flowers.

How are you? she asked, then realised the hollowness of the question. In the stress and relief of her reunion with her son a year beforehand, she had failed to ask or learn anything memorable about this man, although in retrospect she felt she should have.

I'm fine, Anton said, then frowned at the thought that he had answered one meaningless platitude with another one. The market crowds flowed by either side of them as if they were ponderous boulders in a river in spate. The effort required to either terminate or perpetuate the conversation suddenly seemed beyond either of them. They floated and then drowned in this uncertainty.

Then Lucia pulled on Claudia's hand and resolved it with two words: ice cream.

Over their Latte and Machiatto, Anton unwound and gave an authentic answer to Claudia's earlier question: *Well, I've been OK, very much back on the straight and narrow since my difficulties, thanks to your husband, and how is he by the way?*

Claudia tilted her head and lifted a single hand in a gesture of open verdict: they would come to that later.

But then my father died...

Oh, I'm sorry, Claudia said, reaching her hand out a little across the table, and she saw from the moisture in his eyes that the matter was still raw.

It's OK, really, Mrs Reinwald. He was seventy-six, a decent enough age for a man who had survived several heart attacks and a by-pass operation. It's just one of those things we all have to go through...one day.

Claudia's eyes flicked involuntarily to the children, and Vittorrio slurping his strawberry slush-puppy through a multi-coloured straw asked: *Will Daddy die one day, Mummy?*

Oh goodness Vittorrio, not until we're all old, you'll be all grown up by then with a wife and children of your own.

Do you have a wife, Anton? Lucia asked, wide-eyed and Claudia chastised her: *Sweetheart, that's a rude thing to ask.*

Anton suddenly laughed with a light-heartedness that seemed to cheer up everyone around the table. *No, princess. I haven't found the right girl yet, but I will one day, don't worry. It's fun waiting to see who it will be...* He turned around and led her eyes with his hands to consider every face in the crowds streaming past their table. *Look...any one of those girls and ladies strolling by could be Anton's wife one day, isn't that exciting? Look, that one! This one!* The children laughed and became inspired by this game until Claudia had to calm them down.

What about you? Anton asked, *and Franco...?* he said, finding it strange to be using the doctor's first name now.

He could see affection and happiness in her eyes towards him now, but it shifted and receded at her discomfort as the spotlight turned onto herself.

Things have been hard, she began, *we've been working too long hours. Franco...* she began again, then looked meaningfully at the children as if to signal that she couldn't really take the conversation in the direction she wanted it to go. *Well, he could do with more time off. He could do with a friend, like you for instance. He sorts out other people's problems, but I wish he, we, had more time to sort out our own.*

And you? Anton asked, stirring his coffee and fixing her eyes intently.

She raised her eyebrows, as if unclear of the question.

Do you have friends, holidays you can take?

Oh yes, and she snapped out of her reverie as if relieved to have an apparently simple question she could answer. *My friend Vivienne and I...we're taking a walking holiday next week.*

Where? Anton asked.

Into the forest, Claudia replied, *all of it, some of it, an expedition with rucksacks and thermos flasks and tents, just like when we were kids.*

What Anton said next both alarmed and reassured her: *are you going to try to find Leo?*

She had forgotten that Anton had known anything about her brother, and felt suddenly uncomfortable that this deeper motive could be laid bare by a virtual stranger.

Anton saw her disquiet and moved to reassure her. *Your husband told me about him. How he wanders in the forest and writes letters. I'm sorry, I didn't mean to intrude.* He glanced at the children. *It's just...* and he searched Claudia's eyes to see if she had been irrevocably insulted. *Well, this is another of those strange coincidences that keep building up these days.*

Go on... Claudia said, rubbing Lucia's hair with her hands.

Well, you know I was an architect...

No actually, I don't remember if I knew that, or if Franco mentioned it.

Well, I say was, because I resigned my job the day after my father's funeral.

But why? Claudia asked.

I suddenly realised what was important in life. In order to do that maybe you've got to see death at close quarters, ponder what a man's whole life amounts to in the end, before you can look at your own with clear vision and think how to shape it and change it. Life shouldn't be about sweating and slaving in front of a computer all day. It's about fresh air and sunlight and exercise, that's what we've evolved to enjoy, not eating dust and synthetic hamburgers. So I packed it in and applied for a job with the Forestry Council.

Forestry? Claudia asked, surprised.

Yes, I've been getting trained up for the last three months. It's meant a cut in pay but I get free food and lodgings half the time when I'm out on placement. And I'm full of fresh air, up to the brim with all the sunlight I can handle! I'm a forester now.

But that's…wild. I mean well done, congratulations, if that's what you really want to do. You're really sure you'll be happy, are there career prospects, I mean promotions over the years?

Anton laughed out loud again, and now the children were giggling with him before they even understood the joke. *You're not getting it are you? – with all due respect.*

Claudia stared blankly.

Once you breathe the fresh air and spend a few days in the woods and sleep like a log, ha ha ha… the children giggled again like little puppets, *then you realise that money, promotion, careers, overtime, overwork, unhappiness…these are just things you are doing to yourself. Torments, self-imposed. Life isn't about these things. You only really need food and shelter and some honest, preferably physical work, Everything else is…*

Vanity? Claudia suggested, *Extraneous? Unnecessary? Counter-productive?*

Anton still seemed lost for the right word and turned to Lucia who said simply: *Ka-ka.*

Everyone laughed apart from Lucia, as Claudia prepared to take her to the toilet. *Now you stay here with Anton and be good, won't you Vittorrio?*

Uncle Anton. Can we call him Uncle Anton?

Anton laughed again. Claudia paused to ask: *But what was the coincidence, Anton, about you becoming a forester?*

Because I can guide you now, of course. I have access to the right maps and kit and survival training. I can guide you though the forest, I can help you to try and find Leo.

Will you really be able to find Uncle Leo? Vittorrio asked, once his mother and sister had left the table.

Well Vittorrio, I found you didn't I? Anton answered, smiling sweetly.

The night before setting off on their expedition, Vivienne had a dream in which she and Claudia were in a forest made of spider's webs. But with the peculiar half-logic of dreams she was immediately given to understand that all the webs leading off in every direction were somehow the physical legacy of every conversation she had ever had: every one leading out to each person she knew; each of whom was a dim tree trunk wrapped in silk, hidden in the murky distance of sylvan twilight.

As she spoke, she saw that her words were making more spider silk, issuing from her mouth. She flinched and twitched in her growing cocoon, and saw that she was becoming increasingly entwined and encased. Then she realised that her web was connected by a thread to some central monitor: and that up above her a large and many-eyed spider was shuffling along at treetop level. The dream ended as she caught sight through the branches of the creature's black furry legs and several bulbous eyes that were rotating towards her. She noticed to her surprise that the creature wore a Roman Breastplate and clutched a bundle of spears.

★

The doorbell rang and Vivienne answered it sleepily to discover to her surprise that Claudia had brought company. Then she remembered what Claudia had said about having found a forest guide to bring along.

Sorry, slept in, running late again, she said, and fled from the door in mock shame for a moment before halting and returning to shake Anton's hand and introduce herself in uncharacteristically timid style, long dishevelled blonde hair covering her face like jungle creepers.

Had she not been so stunningly beautiful, Anton thought to himself, he might have concluded she was an eccentric social misfit or worse.

When she returned to the living room ten minutes later, fully dressed and packed, he revised his opinion. She seemed in fact, terrifyingly perfect in every sense.

Why are you doing this for us, Anton? What's in it for you? Hoping to get gang-raped in the woods by two dirty old women?

Viv! Claudia exclaimed, but Anton was laughing again in that disarming way of his, as if all of life were a comedy film he could bring to a halt in a second with a quick signal to the director.

Strangely enough, Claudia never really asked me that question, but the reason is probably that Leo intrigues me from what I've heard of him. Maybe I'd like to meet him, or to read some of his letters if you would be so good as to share them with me. Also... Claudia's husband treated me, cured me we should say, after I had some kind of breakdown last year, when I was working too hard. Maybe I'd like to help her and him both now...

And Vittorrio, Claudia added, *Anton, how can you forget to mention that? Remember Viv, I told you someone had led the police to where Vittorrio was? That was Anton.*

Mmm... Vivienne eyed him suspiciously, *you're very open about having had psychiatric help... as indeed I suppose you should be, although this isn't America yet, but there shouldn't be any stigma, should there? In fact, that's commendable, Anton, you seem pretty well adjusted now...*

Well, I realised what actually matters in life recently, and once you get that revelation it's hard to just forget it.

Anton's father died recently... Claudia explained.

In a gesture that amazed everyone, the normally somewhat aloof Vivienne put her hand out and stroked the side of Anton's cheek as if he were a pet dog and whispered: *You poor baby...*

A strange atmosphere filled the room as the two of them held each other's gaze for a moment.

Claudia spoke into the silence at last, out of embarrassment, but the spell wasn't broken yet. Vivienne was stepping backwards as if frightened, unnerved by the inappropriate gesture she had just made. But Anton, unperturbed and still holding her gaze calmly, curiously said: *Do you believe in fate, Claudia?*

Well, it believes in us I would say, Claudia smiled at the door.

Then I should tell you about the dream I had, about Leo in the forest. But it will keep for the journey. Now we should really get on the road I think, we have a long way to travel before nightfall.

★

Driving north through the poorer districts, Vivienne said to Claudia: *You know what Leo would say, don't you? How strange it is that everyone keeps carrying on as if nothing is happening, as if their world isn't going to end...*

   Is that what he writes in his letters? Anton asked.

   I thought Claudia had let you read them?

   Well, the latest one.

   So he could try to pinpoint his whereabouts, Claudia interjected, *from the post mark.*

   Fat chance, we've tried that ruse in years gone by. He's on the move all the time, particularly when he thinks anyone is looking for him.

   How will the world end then? Anton asked, oddly fascinated, *what does he mean?*

   He says Nature is preparing a cataclysm for us, didn't you know? An extinction level event after which the insects or the rhododendrons are going to take over. He says the human spirit is already ebbing away like... what does he call it, Claudia?

   Drawback, I think.

   That's it, you know, like when the tide goes out just before a tsunami comes in.

   Stopped at the lights, Anton tried not to stare too openly at the drunks and drug addicts falling about on the pitiful little park with vandalised benches that constituted the only social centre to this neighbourhood.

   As if guessing his thoughts, Claudia said: *He wasn't, isn't, a snob my brother, Anton. He meant our lot just as much, maybe more. The rich middle-classes, decadent and bored, wife-swapping, bed hopping, depressed, suicidal, rotting from the inside out.*

   So is this mysterious event, the ending of our world, a natural disaster or a man-made one? Does Nature do it to us or do we bring it on ourselves?

   There was a long silence as they drove and then Vivienne said *Both*, quietly, in introspective mood again, *that's his whole point I think, because of Gaia, once you get what he means by that, you realise both can be true at the same time.*

   But can't we do anything to stop it? Anton asked, *Presumably Leo wants us to try to stop it?*

   Ahh... time and causality, that old chestnut. I'm afraid there's a problem with that too, Anton, according to Leo that is. Correct me if I'm wrong Vivienne, but basically Gaia exists outside of time, which means it has access to the future.

   And therefore, Vivienne said into his other ear, taking over: *This catastrophic event in the future whatever it is, has already happened. All we can do is go on driving towards it, like we're on rails.*

   To Hell with that, Anton said, and as if to crystallise the metaphor took an unexpected left turn in search of a short cut to the outskirts.

★

I think you might be labouring under a false assumption, Vivienne said later, eyeing Anton sceptically, before helping him load some of the equipment out of the jeep.

   Yeah? he looked up, running his hands through his hair, a slightly vain gesture which irritated Vivienne.

You're assuming the catastrophic event is a bad thing...

Boy, you are two serious ladies... Anton stood up and laughed. *I thought you said you'd known each other since you were little girls. Did you talk about stuff like this when your pals were playing with Barbie?*

Vivienne made Barbie and Ken play together... Claudia laughed, and Vivienne tutted at an old story being trailed out again, *and made Ken anatomically correct, shall we say, using a bit of black pipe cleaner. She was... quite advanced for her years I think you could say.*

Yeah, and Claudia was amazed when her first boyfriend turned out to have something pink rather than furry and black between his legs.

They fell over laughing, while Anton looked at them both incredulously with his eyebrows raised. *Seriously again...* He said, *seriously now... presumably the end of the world is by definition a bad thing isn't it?*

Only if you're human, Vivienne said, smiling, but growing quiet again.

But we're all there is aren't we? Are chipmunks going to rule the earth, or woodlice?

Nobody rules the earth, Anton, the earth rules us. Maybe we're just a project, like the dinosaurs were. They died out, but life didn't... Claudia said.

Anyway, they didn't all die out. Crocodiles and coelacanths and ferns and horsetail weeds and gingko trees: some things made it through... Vivienne corrected.

The gingko trees survived at the centre of Hiroshima you know, Claudia added, the only living thing that did. *You can't blind a thing that's blind already.*

I read once, Anton said, lifting his rucksack, *that when the British set off the H-bombs on Christmas Island thousands of birds were blinded instantly, left screaming and blind, wondering where they were and what had happened until they slammed into rock or trees.*

A crime against Gaia of the highest order, Leo would say... Vivienne sighed, *maybe even enough to merit the penalty of extinction.*

Hey, you're pretty serious yourself, Anton, what's all this metal gear you've got in the back pack?

Global Positioning System, laptop, satellite uplink, distress flares, infra-red camera.

No shit. You're for real aren't you? Why are we going to carry all that stuff?

Anton stopped and put his pack down. *The views, the fresh air and the wildlife will be stunning I promise you, but once we get into the heart of the forest we will be surrounded by dense woodland for up to seventy five miles in every direction, several days walk to get out of. The forest is vast, Vivienne. If we make a mistake, we die. If we travel carefully and patiently with the right equipment then if we still make a mistake we can at least get helicoptered out.*

Wow, boy scout. You sure talk a good adventure for a reformed pen-pusher. Lead the way, Rambo.

Franco placed his hands on his desk to stop them shaking as he waited for his next patient to enter the room. Why had he allowed her to take this last minute appointment when it would have been so easy to invent some excuse and have her quietly removed from his client list and passed on to a colleague?

But here she was, and to his amazement she was wearing a suit, and apart from the red lipstick and a nose-stud all of her gothic trappings were temporarily gone.

Surprised, Doctor Reinwald? she hovered at the door and he had to flicker his hand in irritation to signal to her to close the door over. Embarrassment: perhaps this was his biggest fear, and the accusation of professional misconduct, and of course his marriage.

She looked good in the suit, and her hair was now long and straight and no longer dyed: revealed as the lovely flaming red she must have been born with.

She sat down in front of him and smiled, searching his eyes for emotion, like reading a magazine. He looked back with all the blankness and bewilderment of a newborn child, and with some difficulty: returned her stare.

Job interview? he asked finally, realising this was not the sort of opening question he would usually start a session with.

Yeah... Veronika sighed, and crossed her legs and took out some cigarettes and matches.

There's no smoking here... Franco said, but numbly and without conviction, like a talking computer, then again:*...this is a non smoking surgery.*

She lit up and leaned back in her seat, eyeing the paintings on the walls, sizing up the place like she might be planning to move in on Monday. *Would you like me to suck your cock?* she finally asked quietly, absent-mindedly, getting bored.

Veronika... did we, did you... use protection... when I was at your house, when I...

When you...? When you what? Oh go on and say it, Doc, when you ejaculated inside my vagina.

He winced, involuntarily.

Oh you were good by the way, vigorous, violent, and let me see, what's the opposite of premature?

That would be the drugs you shot into me, I would imagine, Franco replied, *I suppose there's no point me asking you for the names and molecular compositions of those. Are we playing a word-association game? Laborious?*

Oh... tut, tut, tut... you're too hard on yourself, tiger. Involved was the word I was thinking of, long and involved. There, that's much better.

We're not though are we?

Involved? Well, let me see. It's been,several weeks so I guess by definition that's a no, but then again this casual sex thing is a dangerous game you know: messing with primordial forces. I get the psychic smell of you all over me and visa versa, and then hey presto we wake up thinking about each other, all that sort of shit. That's how it usually goes, isn't it?

What was the job interview for?

Is..., Doctor, I'm going there next, and guess... go on... she smiled, holding her cigarette up over her head.

Sex therapist.

Very good, Doctor, a sense of humour, self-deprecating even. No. An administrative assistant in a lawyer's office. You ready for that blow-job yet?

I hope you don't blow the job, Veronika.

Two jokes in one day, lover. You been popping your own prescriptions?

I hope you get the job and move on. You need to move on. What happened was... I'm sorry, a sordid incident, for which I take some responsibility, despite what

195

was basically an assault on me, I should have known better than to visit you at home. I don't do house calls.

Veronika stood up and wandered around the room then went and lay down on the sofa.

What happened was an aberration... Franco continued, *and it mustn't happen again. You're clearly more or less cured, unless you're going to tell me otherwise, and we don't need to continue your treatment... Veronika?*

Yes, Doctor? she drawled sleepily.

What are you doing?

I'm masturbating of course, Doctor. Clitoral stimulation you'd call it, although I doubt if you've ever discussed it much. As the old joke goes, I've decided to start without you...

Jesus Christ... Franco opened his desk drawer and fumbled frantically for the old key to the door, the one he hadn't had call to use in years. He bounded across the room and managed with some delicacy to lock the door without making enough noise to arouse the suspicions of Rosemary, his middle-aged secretary whose radio was on quietly, tuned to Classic FM.

Veronika, please stop this, he said, standing over her... *get your hands out of there.*

What? she said, *What's the big deal, never see a madwoman jerking herself off on your weekend tour of the asylums?* Her left hand clutched his wrist, and this arm of his in turn was clutching her right wrist, trying to slow her movements. *Crazy woman masturbates in psychiatrist's office... not even a great headline I would say... pretty run of the mill really... you must see shit like this every week you poor devil, no?*

Please stop... he begged. But she pushed his hand lower and he found himself soothing her, curing her, her eyelids fluttering. *Hippocratic Oath...* she muttered, *...you have to alleviate my suffering...*

Running out of breath, she looked more beautiful by the minute, her cheeks slowly taking on the innocent red of ripe apples until the little panicked sounds from her mouth made him lean over and kiss her, still imploring her to stop, swallowing her breaths.

★

The first night in the forest, Anton had a curious dream about Vivienne.

Perhaps it was his instinctive fear of sleeping in the open, but the setting for his dream was an exact mental replica of the clearing where they had gone to sleep, right down to the pine needles and acorns, the rolling hillock beneath the deep shade of the trees, the bark on the thick trunks as fissured as the faces of blind old men.

High up, from out of the canopy of pines, he saw a light then a fluttering butterfly descending in spirals, flitting from tree to tree but somehow growing in size all the time. He felt that the butterfly could sense he was watching it, and sure enough as it grew it made its final descent towards him until six feet high it landed with its wings furled in front of him. He could see it was like a Red Admiral: fabulous patterns of red and black with two emerald eyes that he couldn't discern in the half-light to be either real or decoration. He reached out his hand towards it and the wings of the butterfly slowly and majestically unfurled to reveal the exquisite body of a naked

196

woman underneath. Somehow he sensed this was Vivienne, but her head and neck were buried in some kind of black furry mask, the body of the butterfly itself perhaps. Before he could reach out and touch her flesh, it occurred to him that maybe the naked body was only another disguise, an illusion like eyes on the outside of the wings, and that if he touched the flesh it would not respond like flesh but give way softly and sickeningly, revealing itself as some insect contrivance of feathery tissue. Afraid but fascinated, he held his quivering hand out below her vulva, like offering crumbs to a pet bird, and in time its folds opened and a red tubular tongue distended towards him. Telescopic, it finally revealed within its innermost tube a shining silver needle that pricked his finger and he cried out in his sleep, seeing a great ruby-red teardrop of blood there, winking like a wicked eye.

Next day they encountered a hidden glade by a river where numerous outsized insects flew past them that Claudia marvelled at and took notes and photographs of for her diary: giant dragonflies a foot long, butterflies the side of a fist. Anton trembled at the prescience of his dream but felt unable to share it with his companions.

Pitching a tent and sleeping al fresco was a novelty for the first night, but as the days went by and their rations ran out the hard reality began to set in: physical discomfort and exhaustion and an increasing sense of isolation due to the vast green army of trees around them. Anton tried to keep the journey interesting by relating everything he had learned about tree species: Larch, Cedar, Douglas Fir, their ages and projected heights, here was a stump whose rings revealed it had been planted around the time of the American Civil War. Here were two yews: one female the other male, having sex in slow motion over decades with the aid of every passing breeze. Here was an oak colonised and all but killed by ivy which entirely covered it: keeping its host alive just enough to sustain it.

At first Vivienne and Claudia found his tales of how to catch animals boring and a little childish, until it dawned on them they were going to have to use them soon. *But I'm a vegetarian!* Vivienne exclaimed indignantly.

Not this week you're not, Anton said abruptly as he marched on, *unless you want to die.*

I can eat fruits and nuts! she called after him.

Not enough to sustain the kind of strength you need to keep walking like this, believe me or don't believe me, it doesn't matter, you'll be ripping the squirrel steak out of my hands within forty-eight hours, I guarantee it.

There were rivers of course. He began with fish, easy enough to catch, and baked them in a sand oven made from the embers of their camp fire.

But how on Earth do you think we can find Leo, in a forest this size? Claudia asked, picking fish bones from her teeth as delicately as she could contrive to.

Anton pointed to the fire. *No matter how tough Leo is, and he's obviously pretty tough, he's going to have to light fires now and again. This sector, the one we think he's in, is pretty flat. At dawn and dusk I climb a tree...*

I thought you were just looking for nuts for me... Vivienne laughed.

From any treetop I should be able to see a long way, and I have a telescope. If he's around he must light a fire and we might see him. Then there's tracks. It looks vast and uncharted to the naked eye, but from the maps you can see there are certain logical routes and arteries Leo must take now and again. Fresh water sources for instance. He can't be wandering randomly, despite what he says, or he'd be lost and wouldn't be able to find his way to the various villages where he posts letters. To me that means he has maps, mental ones at least, and he's following routes on which we might find his tracks or other traces, shelters and dug-outs for instance.

After dinner, Anton would sit alone and write his diary while Claudia and Vivienne had time to themselves, talking quietly.

Anton recorded some his first impressions on entering the woods:

Tree bark: like flakes of skin, deeply fissured, twisting over itself, layer upon layer. Uprooted trees; the clay-red soil exposed underneath, rainwater pools forming there. Incredible height of dead-straight pines. Water plummeting through rock pools, rapids, forming grottoes, criss-crossed by fallen trunks, pines growing at the edge of cliffs: blind, the trees don't know the precariousness of their situation and grow regardless. The mosses on the grotto walls: a hundred unnamed species, a botanist's wet dream, soft as sponges to the touch, saturated with rainwater. The rocks underfoot glitter with iron pyrites, fool's gold. Metallic sheen to every wet rock. In the shadow-twilight under the big trees: a hallowed carpet of pine needles leads upwards, vanishing into the morning mist, the roar of a waterfall nearby reverberating through our bones.

He looked up and saw that Vivienne was standing over him. *Here, you said you wanted to read more of Leo's letters,* she said, *here's one I looked out this morning, sort of relevant to our discussion…*

Anton took it and began reading as she walked away:

So through environmental calamity Humanity stands at last on the brink of its own destruction. No. Humanity walks backwards towards the edge of a cliff, while chattering incessantly about the price of oil and other rubbish. No. Humanity, a rather annoying little insect has finally succeeded in making enough noise by jumping up and down on a hot summer's day to rouse the large slumbering creature upon whom it rests, whose blood it sucks, so that the beast is just about to roll over and crush it into pulp. How did we get to this stage? Every life form, every design has its inherent flaws, potentially fatal. Were it not already too late, our first project might have been to map these flaws and use them as a template with which to correct our vision and see beyond the mirror's edge. Here are the five key blindspots of the human brain:-

1.Didactic Thinking. The unconscious presumption that an answer will be simply one thing or the other, black or white. This simplification is always our first approach to a problem, but carries with it the inherent failure to accept complexity and see where multiple factors are at play to produce shades of grey.

2.Projection. The unconscious presumption that other people think like us. This carries with it the consequent failure to recognise, analyse and predict motivations alien or novel to our own, in other words we fail to empathise effectively, because projection is easier.

3.Timeblanking. The unconscious failure to grasp the linear impact of time. A comfortable present, i.e. the day in front of us if pleasant, will always seem more real than the any misfortune which may inevitably arise later out of our actions that day, no matter how dire those consequences, provided they are days, weeks or years hence. Given a combination of danger with time, we tend to ostrich time rather than starting running.

4. Flattery. The social herd instinct of humans pre-programmes us to like those who like us. Thus flattery, entirely regardless of whether it is meant or feigned will completely shut down the critical analytical function of the recipient's brain for an average of two and a half minutes. The effect can only be overcome by extreme self-discipline and extensive practice.

5.Conflation. It is a common philosophical assumption that the human mind is always looking for absolute truth, when in fact it is only programmed to always make the best-fit sense of a situation no matter how little information is available or how flawed the information is. Not making sense of a situation is apparently not an option. To the human mind, a wrong answer is better than no answer. Hence why every tribe on earth has its own elaborate creation myth and accompanying rituals. The range and complexity of modern science should not blind us to the same persistent underlying truth, which has remained unchanged since the days of the caves: it is ludicrous to think that a talking chimpanzee can fully understand the universe that so dwarfs it, the gaps in our knowledge are vast, the inventions we plug those gaps with are only temporary sticking plaster, thus all our 'truths' and assumptions remain wholly unreliable.

Franco found himself crying in the car outside Veronika's house. It had been raining for the last hour and the windscreen wipers were responding on auto-pilot, a mournful little movement, intermittent like a housemaid of the world sweeping up after each fresh calamity. The radio had just announced an earthquake on the other side of the planet in which children had been entombed in their own school. Franco remembered a line from Bob Dylan: just when you think you've lost everything, you find out you can always lose a little more.

The door opened and Veronika sat down on the passenger seat. *As Bugs Bunny used to say, what's up Doc? What's wrong?*

This is wrong, he sobbed. *I can't do this.*

Veronika sighed and put her hand on his knee and said gently: *Look at me.* Then for the first time, she used his first name:

Franco.

He looked up and met her eyes and she held his gaze calmly for a minute, then said: *…Tell me about your childhood.*

Then they both started laughing.

★

On the fourth day travelling, Anton, Claudia and Vivienne found a track not marked on any map. The tyre marks of some unknown off-road vehicle led to a strange clearing in the woods where they found yellow tape tied between trees, as if indicating a crime-scene or tree-felling in progress. But Anton could tell from the silence, the occasional nesting birds, that they were entirely alone and the scene had been abandoned months beforehand. They made their way tentatively past the yellow tape and spread out to explore the area.

Anton heard a whistle from Claudia and made his way back towards her through the thin saplings that were already re-colonising the blighted arena. She seemed apprehensive, and was gesticulating silently towards a strange hillock a hundred yards to her left. Anton approached carefully and circled it, kneeling at its edges to try to understand its meaning.

He could hear the hum of bees from somewhere within the mound, as if a hive was concealed there. Ants were patrolling the perimeter, biting his feet, knees and hands. At the centre, flies were hovering and feeding over what he thought at first was cow dung, but what as his eyes focused through the miasma of noonday heat, seemed to resemble the browning folds of brain tissue, possibly human. From beneath and within this a complex array of electrical wires could be seen leading away in every direction towards the periphery of the mound, where many arrays of batteries lay partially buried in the earth.

Anton backed away carefully, and gestured to Claudia and Vivienne to stay back. *What is it?* they whispered when he returned, and he looked back over his shoulder, troubled and confused.

I honestly don't know, but I don't think we're supposed to be here. There's something unsavoury about this, let's just quietly get out of here, shall we?

You seem rattled, Vivienne said as they reached the yellow tape boundary again.

Maybe you should be, Claudia said from where she stood up ahead reading some sort of notice nailed to a tree. *This says this is a Defence Ministry Restricted Area, Danger Of Death…they do like their hyperbole and melodrama those military boys, don't they?*

Does it say what kind of danger? Anton asked.

Claudia shook her head, *Nothing so helpful I'm afraid, why?*

The one piece of hardware I didn't think to pack was a Geiger counter. Sunburn I can handle, but Leukaemia I could do without contracting on holiday.

Pahhh… Vivienne said, *…Looked like a harmless old pile of electrified dung to me. Could be any number of other silent killers anyway…spores of Small Pox or Anthrax if that's any comfort…*

Just at the moment Claudia yelped and ducked as a particularly large dragonfly buzzed past her head like a model helicopter. *What the…*

Jesus…that one's practically back to Jurassic proportions, Anton gasped, fumbling for his camera.

They all watched as the creature approached the cordoned zone, slowed and hovered uncertainly, then diverted its path in a different direction.

The children had been badly behaved in the morning, too much energy and mischief in the air, as if the departure of their mother on holiday was a green light for an adventure of their own.

Now Imelda, the Reinwalds' housekeeper, having carefully tired them out in a lunchtime game in the park, sat Vittorrio and Lucia down in the study with various games and puzzles in the hope that they would play quietly or get bored and take an afternoon nap.

They sat on their little chairs and eyed the marble chessboard on the table between them. The study was the finest room in the house: original oak panelling to dado height and oil paintings on the wall above, polished wooden floorboards on which the children scuffed their shoes now, swinging their feet between the chairs.

Vittorrio took the ivory and ebony chess pieces from the box and began to set them up as his sister watched.

Why do they go that way? she asked

It's how papa sets them up, he showed me.

Which one's the Queen. Can I go the Queen?

There's two queens, silly, the black and the white. You don't go the Queen, you go black or white.

Is that her?

No, that's the Knight.

But it's a horse, not a night, is it the Queen's horsey?

Maybe, it's called a Knight, like a knight in armour, you know, jousting and all that stuff, it's a tradition, it's the rules.

Did Papa teach you all the rules, do you remember them?

I think so. But I guess we can make new rules if we get bored. The Knight can do things none of the other pieces can. Look, he's allowed to jump over other people and move in a funny L-shape like this...

Why?

It's just the rules, since ages ago, since Vikings and stuff, since the Stone Age. All the other pieces have to shuffle around a step here or there, forward or diagonal, but the Knight gets to jump.

What does this one do? Lucia asked, her hand on a Castle.

That's called the Whistle. You pick it up and blow through the hole on top of it and see how many Pawns you can blow over.

Lucia giggled, *And this one?* she said, holding up a Bishop.

See that roundy shape? Vittorrio continued earnestly, *that's called the Stishup. You put him up your nose and hold your head over the chessboard and wait until you sneeze, cos that's him condemning them to death.*

Lucia was excited now, clapping her hands together: *What happens to the pieces that die?*

They just go back in the box until the next game of course, Vittorrio mused, puzzled by her curiosity.

No blood? No hanging or beheading? she whispered conspiratorially.

Vittorrio smiled mischievously and leaned down over the board until their two noses pressed together, sharing a secret. *Have you got a hacksaw?*

After he had cooked everyone a dinner of roast rabbit, Anton went to sit on his own on a hillock at the edge of a clearing, leaving Vivienne and Claudia to talk quietly together by the fire. The sound of the evening birds and chirping crickets where he sat drowned out whatever they were saying. The lowering sun turned blood red like a throbbing heart, a solitary eye that looked into his soul. In the heart of the wilderness at last, he had nowhere left to hide. His mind emptied, he lost all track of time for a while, until he realised Vivienne had come and sat down quietly beside him.

What are you thinking about? she asked, then added more softly: *Your father?*

No, I believe he's part of me now. In some ways he feels closer now than when he was alive. There's not a tribe on earth who don't believe something similar. Not a religion in the history of the planet that hasn't suggested this, until now of course. Our religion of science, handy for opening a tin of soup, but not for making any coherent or useful sense out of the business of life and death, is it?

Pahhh... Vivienne snorted, *Science built your jeep and your laptop and your GPS, that's all useful isn't it?*

Only, ultimately, if it makes people happier. Are you sure that it does?

No. Not sure. Vivienne said quietly, after a while.

So I don't miss him...because he's part of me, he's looking out from inside my eyes right now.

Maybe if I knew Leo was dead, I could feel closer to him, maybe that's my problem... Vivienne looked down at the ground, digging at it with a stick.

The sun seemed to shift a notch lower and redder, the flies rose up in clouds from the marsh. They turned and looked at each other. *And what does your father see through your eyes now?*

Vivienne... Anton looked away into the distance, *you are a beautiful woman...but what's the point in all of this?*

This?

Men and women, animals and plants, wind and water and trees. What does it all want? You've seen it all on this journey: the bears hunt the wolves who hunt the wild cats who hunt the mice...it's all carnage and copulation and child-rearing. But what does it all amount to that's of any consequence? What does God or Gaia want of us? Just birdsong and peacock feathers, reproduction and flowering? Aren't you ever tired of this pointless cycle, what does it all lead to? Just our own extinction or some marvellous future of space travel and dreams? Either way we won't see one bit of it, we'll be dust. So why bother? Just how and why should we keep going?

For the beauty of it of course, Vivienne sighed, *...the ongoing revelation of beauty. Pain, horror, joy, hope...they're all just colours in the palette, light and shade, life and death, the colours without which the picture of life could have no beauty, it would just be grey mist. Leo said these answers can only be felt, not understood...*

Felt, not understood? What does that mean? Where does that get us? And he's not here. Where did it get him?

Vivienne put her hand on Anton's forearm: *He said you must acquire the grace of an animal, the innocence of a child, to understand. A total lack of self-consciousness.*

And how do we do that?

Pay attention... she said and then leaned closer and kissed him.

Imelda checked in on the children again and was pleased and amazed to see that they were apparently enthralled in a game of chess. She hovered at the door unnoticed, such was their concentration.

What's happening now? asked Lucia, their two faces lowered like vast moon and sun over the bloody battlefields of their minds.

The Queens have made all their moves and all the pawns are gone. They were in the open, but now your queen is trapped by her defences.

What can happen next? Are any moves possible?

I'm not sure, it might be stalemate.

Checkmate?

No, that's different, that's when we trap and kill the kings, but they're both still free and just wandering about.

Can the knight save the Queen? Make a way out for her?

Maybe…but there are two knights remember, I've been keeping mine in reserve, hidden away out of sight. I might bring him forward to challenge yours.

A jousting match?! Lucia clapped her hands. *Beheadings?*

Running back in the twilight to meet Claudia, Anton fought the rush of adrenalin and endorphin in his veins, the impact of pheromones and oxytocin, the demeaning predictability of his body's reaction to making contact with another.

I hate this, he said to Claudia, smiling strangely, as he found her at the river's edge, light in her hair, turning round to look at him. *It's like some third rate teen movie, where Vivienne and I are supposed to get all gushy now while you play gooseberry and get lonelier. Jesus, why are we so trapped inside our biology, so incapable of being more?*

Anton, what are you havering about?

Forgive my impertinence, but I seem to have got to know you and your family through some kind of divine accident of fate and I can see you're not happy in your marriage…

Her eyes fell. *Ohhh…what has Viv been saying to you?*

Nothing, nothing at all. I'm just talking about what I see with my own eyes, and it feels weird not to talk about it. I think you should, and we should.

Anton, you're very sweet, but I don't want to off-load all my private complications on you.

No, no, what I'm saying is that I've grown to like you, Claudia, respect you and like you very much. I want you to be happy and for things to work out for you. I don't want to be the agent of anything that makes you unhappy.

Her eyes were soft and full of sadness and something approaching love now, as she stood and looked back at the babbling idiot Anton seemed to have become.

Vivienne had caught up with them now, her skin glowing, her long golden hair blowing back over her shoulders, her head thrown back in laughter at first but then unsure whether Anton was joking or serious. Claudia looked halfway between enchanted and horrified.

I feel like a character in a novel who's about to punch the author, Anton said, looking at them both uncertainly. *Fuck it*, he said at last, and grabbed Claudia and kissed her passionately on the lips.

Fuck it, he said again, muttering madly to himself as he turned away from both of them, almost angry, stomping off. *I'm supposed to be helping you find your brother and your husband. Two married women, maybe one of them a widow, the other one's husband's just saved my sanity a year ago, what kind of a way is this to show gratitude? This is nuts*, he sighed, sitting down on a tree stump to talk to the long grasses.

But he heard a swishing noise and a splash behind him that brought him to his senses. Vivienne's clothes lay hanging from various trees. She had thrown herself into the river.

Jesus, what now... he said and got up and headed after her, with Claudia following at his side, but they both slowed down as they reached a rock outcrop and saw that she was swimming happily and safely among the water lilies.

He turned to look at Claudia as if waking from a dream and saw that her eyes were kind and mocking, reflecting a glowing blue twilight that now seemed to be permeating everything, as if moving through their bodies, making them translucent like fish.

She stood in front of him and unbuttoned his shirt as they both started laughing. With the immediacy and innocence of children, blinded by the heartbeat of the sunken sun, they moved hand in hand into the pure moment, slipping into the silken water.

The grace of animals! Anton shouted to Vivienne after the first shock of the cool water had exhilarated him, and she laughed back as they swam to meet her. Silver diadems of light, swaying reeds and lilies circled and brushed past them, enfolding them. Countless unfamiliar textures caressed them in a kaleidoscope of touch. Without clothes, the world changed, they changed. They all three embraced and frolicked in the water in a way that was entirely chaste to them, but which might have aroused a more cynical observer. With their ardour neutralised by cold and tiredness, they were able to fondle each other, even their genitals in a way that was only friendly and hilarious. They were laughing at being human.

They had walked nearly twenty miles that day. When they returned to the glowing embers of their campfire they were so tired and refreshed and shorn of care that they simply fell asleep naked together, entwined, under one blanket. The question of the logistics of who might be contemplating sex with anyone else would have to wait until the morning.

Vittorrio opened his soldier chest and brought out a dozen of his favourites: one to thirty-second scale plastic Romans with tin alloy bases, red fibre plumes and shiny metallic shields. He carefully laid them out on the chequerboard in among the remaining chess pieces.

What rule is this now? his sister asked, a little sceptically.

When two bishops get taken straight after each other, you are allowed to supplement both sides' forces, you know like reinforcements.

But how will we know which ones are yours and mines? Whose black and white?

Surprised by his sister's practicality, Vittorrio reluctantly had to face that he hadn't addressed this issue, and thought on his feet instead like a true politician: *Neither. They're a third force. Like UN Peacekeepers except they're totally up for it.*

We can't have three sides, we'd need to get Imelda in to play for them.

Yes, we can have three sides. There were three sides at Waterloo. There were three sides in the Balkan wars, Daddy said they had Serbs and Croats and Muslims and Albanians...

204

That's four.

Well, it was complicated. We'll keep our war simple, promise. Now, let's throw the dice to see what the Romans do...

★

The moon cleared the clouds for a moment and revealed a figure, crouched among the highest branches of a cedar, hunched and patient, watchful, immensely still. His breath sighed in indiscernible harmony with the woods around him as he surveyed the small campsite below him. Such was his camouflage it would have been impossible to guess his identity now, even to those who might have known him once, nor possible to tell if the weapon clutched at his shoulder was a rifle or a spear. The clouds shifted to clothe the moon once more and he was gone, returned to the background of bark and leaf like a chameleon, a dream forgotten by a child waking on the first day of summer.

Douglas Thompson's short stories have appeared in a wide range of magazines, most recently *New Writing Scotland* and *Chapman*. His first book, *Ultrameta* (Eibonvale Press) was published in 2009 and his second novel *Sylvow* (whose chapters, like this one, have been popping up in *Ambit* over the last two years) will appear in autumn 2010 (also from Eibonvale). www.glasgowsurrealist.com/douglas.

Beverley Bie Brahic

On Stendhal's Pants

Stendhal, my dear, you were saying
as we jogged that evening to the pond
(fireflies fizzing in the leaves)
would scribble his thoughts around the waistband
of his pants, in hopes, you said, his words
would rub off on his skin. 'Around
his trousers?' I clarified. 'You don't think
he wore underwear?' Your brow arched.
Flustered, I let the matter drop.

Esprit d'escalier. What I wish I'd said
is that my reading of 18th century erotic tales,
a plumpish volume whose Watteau cover girl
perches, skirts hitched, on a spindly chair
astride a gentleman who, for all I know,
may be deep in thought, about the supper,
which was excellent, or the music
which accompanied it – unless, that is,
the gentleman's a scribbler attending
to the friction of his words against his skin
(as an oyster tends its grain of sand) –
makes me think in those days no one
wore underwear, that delightful
complication not unlike the lacy
clauses that defer thought's resolution –

although, dear scholar, I confess
this could be a case of wishful thinking
on the part of Gentle Reader, prompt –
too prompt? – to take words for reality.

How do I Love Thee?

First and last, your skin,
the long bones (*off with pyjamas!*)
of your legs unwinding
taut sheets. Two, the throb
of your human meat
when I lurch up at 3 o'clock
wrestling monsters, Hydra-headed
in the dark: dawn as yet
unfledged, I plummet
down the shaft, heart trapped
at the roof of my mouth again.

Again, your back's sore, head
aches from work, and me, gut
in knots with impatience, and remorse
for words of comfort
lodged like a wishbone in my throat,
I fling into the pan a pair
of chops, pinch of salt, sprig
of sage (*salvia officinalis*), wine
clear as this glass I raise
to skin and bones I crave
all the hours of the night.

Beverley Bie Brahic is the author of a poetry collection, *Against Gravity* (Worple Press) and ten translations from the French, most recently Hélène Cixous's *Hyperdream* (Polity) and a selection of Francis Ponge poems, *Unfinished Ode to Mud* (CBeditions), shortlisted for the 2009 Popescu Prize for European Poetry in Translation. A Canadian, she lives in Paris, and Stanford, California.

Chris Pig

Scenes from Domestic Life

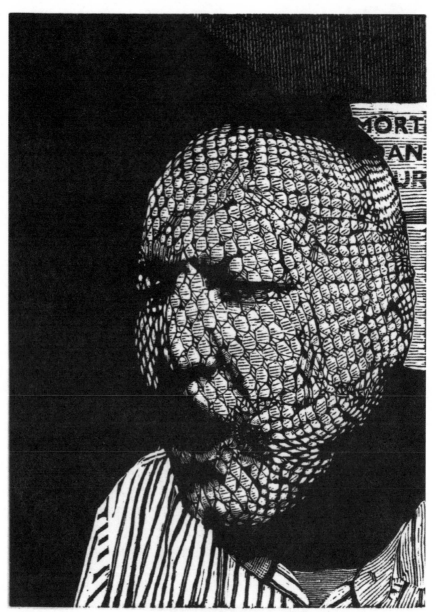

Nobody move!

Magda the duck-billed
Georgian lady

No-Knickers Tony

There goes Madge with
her fledgelings

Sand Gammon

Tyre Man

Weren't doin nuffink

Kitten's tea party

G 20

Chris Pig moved back from Cordoba, now lives in Hackney.
www.chrispig.com

Poems from the Past

In early numbers of *Ambit*, we published a 'poem from the past'. The idea (mine, I suppose), was that we should acknowledge how much many 'good' poems had been published and subsequently ignored. Now *Ambit* will introduce the series again but this time with four from *Ambit*'s own past. The first is 'Looking for McDonagh' by Jack Marriott, which appeared in *Ambit* 10, a special Manchester number. Jack published far too little – I have one pamphlet – but this opened the issue. It caught the 'lost' feeling of Manchester, a city into which you disappeared. The second is 'The Philosophical Poem' by Gavin Ewart, with illustrations by Mike Foreman. Gavin strangely never collected this poem and I drew his attention to this shortly before his died. It shows all his skills – marvellous rhyme schemes and rhythms, the vernacular language, the jokiness (but underneath the jokes a deep seriousness). Three is 'That Beauty, This Beast' by Edwin Brock, from *Ambit* 151. This is also an uncollected poem. It shows all Edwin's obsessions, his tormented psychosexual relationships, but linked to this an awareness of his place in a tormented world – footprints in the snow all over Europe. Finally, the fourth is 'A Richard Lovelace Situation' by Julia Casterton from *Ambit* 73. Julia was much admired for the time she devoted to her own poetry and the skill with which she taught it. This striking piece on football and drinking shows her great talents in rambunctious style.

Jack Marriott
Looking for McDonagh

Here, somewhere, McDonagh lives;
He has been seen by a common thief,
Strutting the slum, his hands held
As in prayer, and that tweed collar
Turned up ragged against the weather.
And so, this rain, I walked strange streets
And move through passing dialogues
Perhaps to see again McDonagh.
But no one knows him, or so they say –
Although I almost described him –
His well-trimmed beard and leather Bible
And his love of girls against the wall.
And all his songs in street-lamp yellow,
Bawdy holes in the fog when time was called.
The women deny they ever knew him
And have no gossip of his wife
(High breasts, a temper, a strong right arm).
She gave him a backward child and no rest
Since brass-band summers as a youth

He swaggered grass with fag and book;
A ballad of a boy. Some said a saint
And by that meant he could sin with grace.
Saint McDonagh, somewhere here and none to tell.
Or will not. His father's son (but still No)
Whose father courted an Irish girl
But married in Chapel and died in drink
To the rattle of tambourines. The wall
Ahead is chalked God…The Queen
And a Chester's pub is across the road.
This could be McDonagh's place. Or Joe's.
(His brother, tall as Dad and celtic;
And now a labourer with a gammy arm.)
But the pub, though full of Saturday,
Warm with week-end and willing flesh,
Holds no McDonagh. Yet the landlord
Thinks he knows the man. A noisy swine –
And barred; these bloody Irish.
(Though born in 'Cheetham's Jewish'
And taught that Love is grey; his
Mother's God, and to hell with him.)
A drink and back to the drizzle
To look for himself again.
Rain takes me back to his vision
(Idle or perhaps too real)
Where he saw himself in blinding prison
Pulling petals from the sun.
And the time my mother woke me after twelve
To say goodbye before she died
And I walked the streets with McDonagh
Till the Nelson opened its doors.
And when Gwyn missed and then mis-carried
He was the best man and mourner.
                    Noise, carried
Across the croft, brings me back to Salford
And the search for my youth again.
Yet perhaps it's best if I never find him –
Perhaps he did go mad (or worse, went sane)
And now says Mass or drinks hellfire
In Jehovah's dereliction. The wrong
things happen to the right men, often.

And so I leave Whit Lane, alone;
But in the rain, as in a poem,
I swear I hear McDonagh's song.

Gavin Ewart
The Philosphical Poem

In the ocean where a squid is a squid
the smallest lifeman is a mychtophid,
like us
he lives in a huge anonymous crowd,
he's one of a million, he isn't proud,
on a 19 bus

he would be meekly paying his fare
from here to the metaphysical there;
he's too
small for the sharks to bother about.
No operatic scream or tenorial shout
or the local zoo

will feature him or deplore his death
and what he draws is hardly breath,
as we
in our cigarette-laden rooms
wait for the prophesied Doom of Dooms,
the encroaching sea

finally left in entire command.
The US Army may rule the land
but how
could it fight in a nuclear/chemical war
where the rich as well as the pitied poor
get theirs fast – right now!

Saxon buildings had towers and quoins,
we are preoccupied with our loins,
but all
History crumbles, and pretty quick,
the softwet quim and the standing prick;
and no Roman wall

can keep the barbarian gas at bay.
The centuries taught us to hope and pray,
who knows
if the children that we photograph
will survive what the wiseacre polymath
prophesies? What grows
will grow down as well as up:

the three-legged cur was once a pup,
the rose
will die as every summer dies.
Permanences are just white lies
and the time-trained nose

can smell decay in the tightest bud.
Something crawled out of the lukewarm mud
at first –
the cumbersome reptile (even wings!)
became the colourful bird that sings.
If you have a thirst

for the glory that every hero gets
and the glamour that glows round historians' pets,
just think
how you could end in the earth or the sea.
For you and you and you – and me –
our bright printer's ink

might not exist to record our deeds.
You might be out of sight under the weeds
or bits
of you might float on the empty air.
No shouting crowds – and an empty chair
where the Leader sits!

Edwin Brock
This Beauty, That Beast

It is that moment
in a story or poem
when he goes
for the first time, alone,
to her room

and the fantasies
that have seen you through
your life begin.

There is the locked door,
white sheets upon
a single bed,
fireglow and footprints
in the snow all over Europe

as though crossing these frontiers
this touching overcomes
inheritance and language.

There are the words
you cannot hear
(there is always something
before the first thing
you remember) and the
beckoning which disturbs
like an interrupted dream.

You do not enter
the spider is on the wall,
the eyeless teddy-bear
by your side): barefoot
upon the same cold stair
you strain to hear
the breathing of an Eden
you did not know
and cannot share.

Julia Casterton
A Richard Lovelace Situation

> *'My old man said Be a City Fan*
> *and I said Bollocks You're a Cunt.*
> *I'd rather shag a bucket with a big hole in it*
> *than be a City fan for just one minute…'*

That's all I can remember of the words
but we sang them for a long time
with the United fans in La Coruña.

Chris was winding them up, saying they'd lose 4–0
and maybe, maybe, a few fists tightened.
But before anything bad could happen

Lloyd came and made us sit down.
Sit Down, yer Deportivo cunt, he said. I'm Lloyd,
and I'm United. Una cerveza for this cunt here

and a café con leche for his missus.
Stein, his twelve-year-old son, was there as well
and Lloyd said they'd just come from a brothel

where 300 United fans had been with gorgeous women
for 60 Euros apiece. Stein called it a Broth.
I said it's a Brothel, but he preferred Broth.

Chris asked Lloyd where United stood
in his list of priorities, and Lloyd said
I Am United. It comes before my wife,

before my son here – and I'd kill for him.
Then he started to cry, and said he felt a bit funny.
Well, my job comes first, he said,

but that's only so I can go to United every week.
And Chris said, So you're telling me
you love United more than you love your wife,

and Lloyd wept and said he did.
The barman smiled and nodded, Lloyd ordered
one more round and then we all staggered

to the Riazor Stadium. We got separated, then,
Lloyd to the United section, we to find
the seats the tout had sold us

five hours before.
        Chris fell down
four times, and the Red Cross had to
sort him out. They suggested a brain scan

but I was tired after the match
(which Man United won 2–0)
so I marched him back to the hotel,

and put him to bed.
Then I opened a bottle of Tempranillo
and toasted Lloyd, and toasted Stein.

And I toasted Lloyd's wife
who has a cunt who loves her.
Who could not love her quite so much

did he not love United more.
And at the moment I went out like a light
in the Hotel Nido, La Coruña.

Mike Barlow

Midnight Dipper

Last night the bets were on me: whether I'd make it back.
This morning my mate came round to split his winnings:
20 quid at three to one. What else are friends for? They
must have slipped me something to give odds like that.

I left the bar to a skinful of cold air. From then on I've
only their word for it they stuck like sleuths, watched me
trip and stagger, plonk myself on the bonnet of a BMW
and bang on about astronomy and the ethics of the lottery.

It must have been a long route home via the town centre
where I spewed at the feet of Victoria Regina then
slipped in my own mess. At the lights a girl in a skimpy
blouse saw me across, one arm round my waist, a small
hand deftly fishing my back pocket.

At least when I got to the door I found the right key
while those two hid in the ginnel until the hall light signalled
money could change hands. I'll not let on I came to on
the kitchen floor naked as a flounder or that the wallet
they retrieved from midnight's dipper was a good wad
thicker than mine.

Manna

As rumour follows storm, word got round:
a freighter grounded, crated cargo
washed up and ours for the picking.
A wheelbarrow stacked to tottering height
with surgical gloves and shower caps,
then a boy from the Creek estate
wheeling a silver Kawasaki up the street,
frame and two wheels, no tank. A neighbour
handed out bird tables, survival equipment
should we at last be driven to a diet
of finches and robins. Ironing boards, televisions,
kites, ornamental garden barrels. Cookery books.
Lorry loads. The coming and going.
Where from, where to, a mystery.
Our bypassed town with its silted harbour,

its quarrymen on half time, a sudden Klondike,
all night traffic of traffickers, an invasion
of transits, trailers, trucks and cattle boxes,
the shed skins of fast food littering
gutters, choking drains. We're a hungry town
at the end of the day, at the end of the line,
but as St Peter might have said to the couple
going nowhere, their pick-up axle deep in shingle,
there's only so much you can do
with fifteen 20 metre rolls of deckchair fabric.

Mike Barlow won the National Poetry Competition in 2006. He has two full
collections, *Living on the Difference* (Smith/Doorstop, 2004) and *Another Place*
(Salt, 2007). His pamphlet *Amicable Numbers*, a winner in the 2008 Templar
Pamphlet Competition, was a Poetry Book Society Pamphlet Choice.

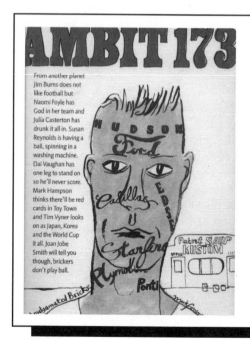

From another planet
Jim Burns does not
like football but
Naomi Foyle has
God in her team and
Julia Casterton has
drunk it all in. Susan
Reynolds is having a
ball, spinning in a
washing machine.
Dai Vaughan has
one leg to stand on
so he'll never score.
Mark Hampson
thinks there'll be red
cards in Toy Town
and Tim Vyner looks
on as Japan, Korea
and the World Cup
it all. Joan Jobe
Smith will tell you
though, brickers
don't play ball.

**AMBIT No. 173
Tim Vyner comes on
board as our first sports
correspondent, Julia
Casterton also into sport
in Spain and Naomi
Foyle, also into sport,
records that yes, foot-
ballers are sexy.**

Emily Berry

David

The hand that writes is the executive hand,
says Nurse Glory. We're writing postcards
at the Stazione di Santa Maria Novella.

The other is the bad hand! she warns.
In case I forget I write *MY BAD, GLAD HAND*
on the back of my left, but the ink runs;

I'm sweating. When we walk the streets
of Europe's cities Nurse Glory's executive hand
keeps hold of my bad because I am untrustworthy.

Sometimes she lets her own bad hand slap me
and then she makes a fist with her good hand
and bites it and looks terribly contrite. In Hamburg

she marched me up and down the Reeperbahn
shouting: *This is what becomes of bad girls!* I'm not
absolutely the most hopeless case she's ever had

on her sainted hands, Nurse Glory says, but mercy,
I'm not far off. *Dear Doctor*, my postcard begins.
My correspondence with the Doctor is strictly

confidential. As a result, I never write to anyone else.
*I'm writing to you with my executive hand. Today
we said goodbye to the Duomo and the Ponte Vecchio.*

Phew-ee! It's hot, and sad. I miss you. Love, Me.
The picture on the front is of Michelangelo's David,
which Nurse Glory forbade me to see. Like all

mental health professionals, she's obsessed with
genitalia. *P.S.*, I add, *David's ball-sack looks like an
upside-down heart*. My innocence is really incredible.

Emily Berry won an Eric Gregory Award in 2008 and her pamphlet, *Stingray Fevers*, was
published the same year by tall lighthouse. She is currently co-writing a book about
breakfasts called *The Breakfast Bible*, to be published by Bloomsbury in 2011. She has
recently received an Arts Council grant to help her complete her first poetry collection.

Kit Wright Highgate '09

Please enter my subscription to Ambit
UK £28, Rest of Europe £30/€44, Rest of World £32/$64

Single copies
UK £7.50, Rest of Europe £9/€15, Rest of World £10/$20

Price differences reflect postage costs.
Currency exchanges include bank charges, which can be
avoided by subscribing via our website. Institute prices
and archival issue prices available on request. Ambit is
published quarterly in January, April, July and October.

Name / Address (CAPS)

Method of payment

I enclose a cheque for the sum of:

made payable to AMBIT. *Please note: Cheques are only*
acceptable in Sterling or US Dollars.

OR Please charge my Visa/Mastercard
delete as appropriate

the sum of:

Card number:

Signature:

Card expiry date:

From UK post this form free to:
AMBIT, FREEPOST ND 6008, LONDON N6 5BR
From Overseas post to:
AMBIT, 17 Priory Gardens, LONDON N6 5QY, UK

Supported by
ARTS COUNCIL
ENGLAND

CONTENTS

Futures

Ambit 201. Our hard copy Index of numbers 150 to 200 will be out in July. Browse through to identify your favourite Ambit authors and Artists. Ambit 202 out in October has a mass of material held over from 200. Texts from N. F. Simpson and an especial selection from Fred Voss of poems from the factory. More Foreman drawings. Never miss out on Ambit. All the best Martin Bax

ISSN 0002-6972

£10